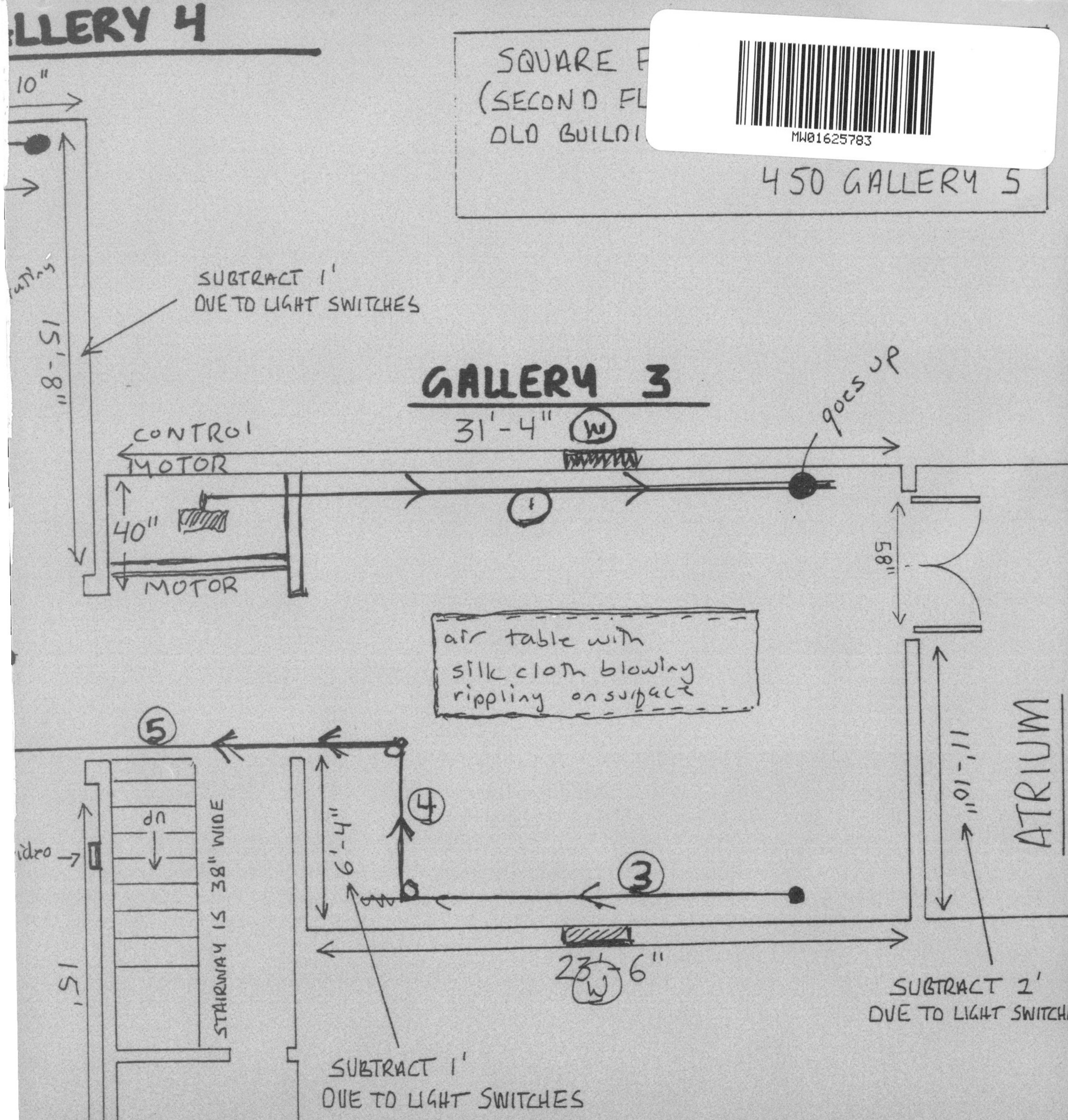

GALLERY 4
10"
SQUARE F
(SECOND FL
OLD BUILDI
450 GALLERY 5
MW01625783
SUBTRACT 1'
DUE TO LIGHT SWITCHES
15'-8"
GALLERY 3
31'-4"
W
CONTROL
MOTOR
goes up
40"
MOTOR
58"
air table with
silk cloth blowing
rippling on surface
5
4
3
dn
STAIRWAY IS 38" WIDE
video
6'-4"
11'-10"
ATRIUM
15'
23'-6"
W
SUBTRACT 2'
DUE TO LIGHT SWITCHES
SUBTRACT 1'
DUE TO LIGHT SWITCHES

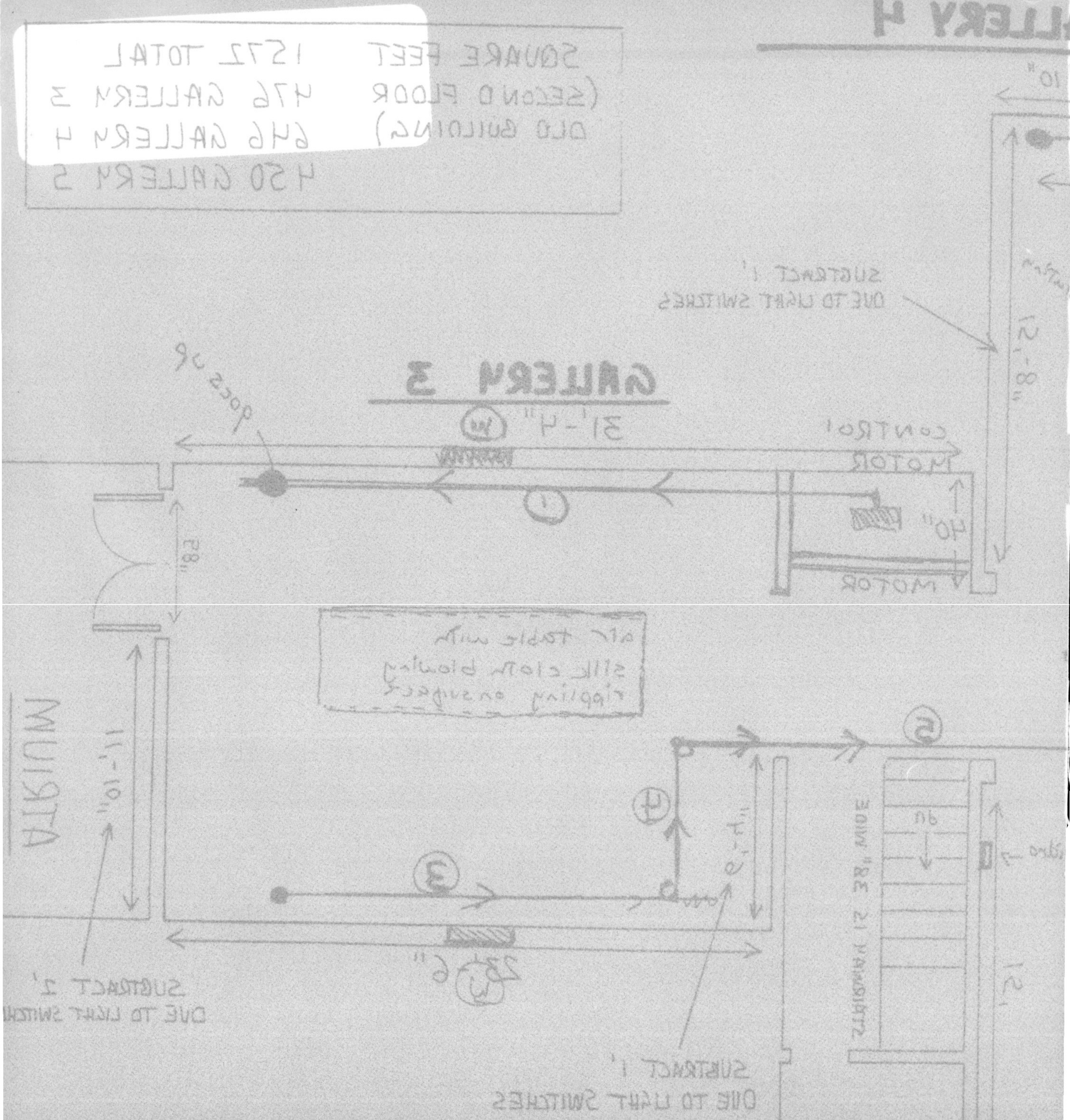

SQUARE FEET
(SECOND FLOOR
OLD BUILDING)
1572 TOTAL
476 GALLERY 3
646 GALLERY 4
450 GALLERY 5
GALLERY 3
31'-4"
CONTROL
MOTOR
MOTOR
40"
15'-8"
SUBTRACT 1'
DUE TO LIGHT SWITCHES
air table with
silk cloth blowing
rippling on subject
ATRIUM
11'-10"
SUBTRACT 2'
DUE TO LIGHT SWITCH
23'-6"
6'-4"
SUBTRACT 1'
DUE TO LIGHT SWITCHES
STAIRWAY IS 38" WIDE
up
15'

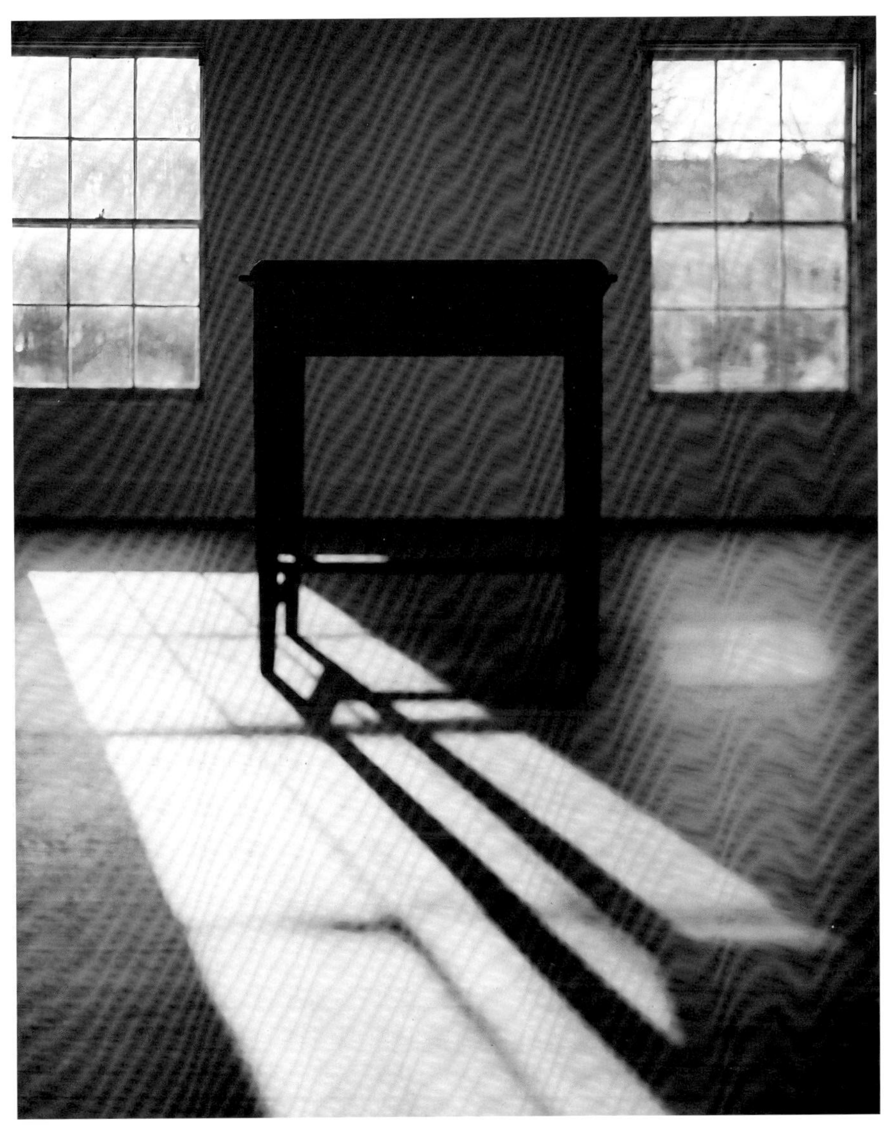

A portion of The Aldrich Museum's general operating funds has been provided through a grant from the Institute of Museum and Library Services, a Federal agency serving the public by strengthening museums and libraries.

Exhibition and education funding provided, in part, by the Connecticut Commission on the Arts.

Education funding provided by: The Alexander Julian Foundation for Aesthetic Understanding and Appreciation, The O'Grady Family Foundation, The Perrin Family Foundation, and The RJR Nabisco Foundation.

ISBN: 1-888332-09-3

258 Main Street, Ridgefield, Connecticut 06877
Telephone 203 438-4519

Design: Marcus Ratliff, New York
Composition: Amy Pyle
Imagesetting: Center Page
Printing: V & L Printers

Ann Hamilton

whitecloth

The 1998 Larry Aldrich Foundation Award Exhibition

January 24 – May 23, 1999

The Aldrich Museum of Contemporary Art

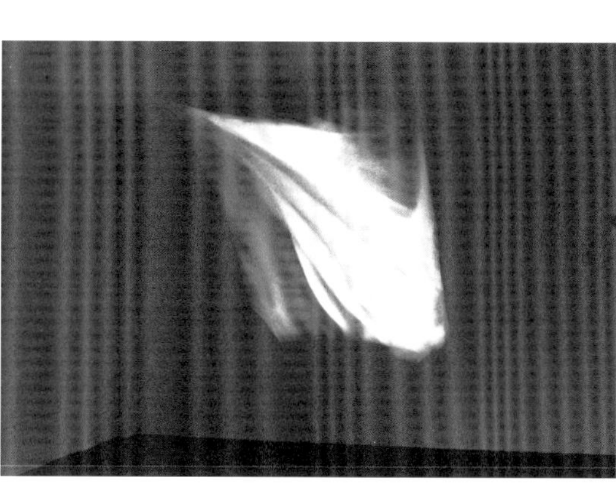

Acknowledgments

Harry Philbrick
Director

There is a long list of people whose hard work, skill, generosity, ingenuity, and dedication have enabled the Museum to achieve its goal of realizing Ann Hamilton's *whitecloth*. At The Aldrich, Richard Klein (most especially), the Dream Team (Jonathan Bodge and Amos Prahl), Mary Kenealy, and the entire show change crew worked miracles. The degree of daily involvement throughout the exhibition from The Aldrich staff may not be readily apparent to viewers; it is, however, deeply appreciated by both Ann and the Museum. Heide Hendricks, Nina Carlson, Lynda Carroll, Rafe Churchill, Paul Harrick, Kay Usher, Robin Phillips, Barbara Toplin, Wendy Moran, Jessica Hough, Jennifer Millet-Barrett, Suzanne Enser-Ryan, and Anne Murphy deserve special thanks for everything from working midnight hours to allowing the conference room to sound like an earthquake. To Rafe, Kay, and Anne Murphy for ongoing sewing, thank you; to Anne Murphy for helping with young Emmett and Clara, thank you; to Heide for letting her office take on the qualities of an airliner, thank you (you deserve frequent flier miles at the very least); to Lynda and Jonathan for still and digital photography, thank you.

Cliff Moran was of great help, as always; so too was David Gelfman. Their skill and responsiveness is greatly appreciated. Zach Hadlock was a tremendous help, his quiet hard work, insight, and skill were essential to the project.

At Perfection Electricks of New York, our thanks go to Marty Chafkin, Eric Radocchia-Carlson and Alex Radocchia-Carlson, Stewart Tygert, and Don Reickles. Eric and Alex deserve special thanks for their many follow-up visits. Rich Mitchell and Amelia Rodriguez at Baxter Healthcare Corporation (Round Lake, Illinois) were instrumental in achieving the "water wall."

We are also very grateful for the insightful and beautiful writing of Ann Lauterbach and Nancy Princenthal, whose involvement in this project illuminates it so well.

Maria Troy, Paul Hill, Amanda Ault, Bonita Makush, and Rachel Wilkins in the Art and Technology Program at The Wexner Center for the Arts, Ohio State University, helped Ann with the videos. Shawn Scully lent his photographic patience and skill to the pinhole images. April Posey constructed and polished the mirror collar until Ann was sure her fingers must nearly have worn away. At Ann's office and studio, special thanks to Brinda Woods and Kristine Miller Helm. Special thanks to Sean Kelly and all the staff at his gallery in New York.

I would like to particularly acknowledge Michael Mercil and Jane Philbrick for their inestimable help and patience, and Emmett and Clara, who breathed their own vigor into this endeavor.

And most of all, thank you Ann Hamilton. It has been a joy and a privilege to work with you.

Introduction

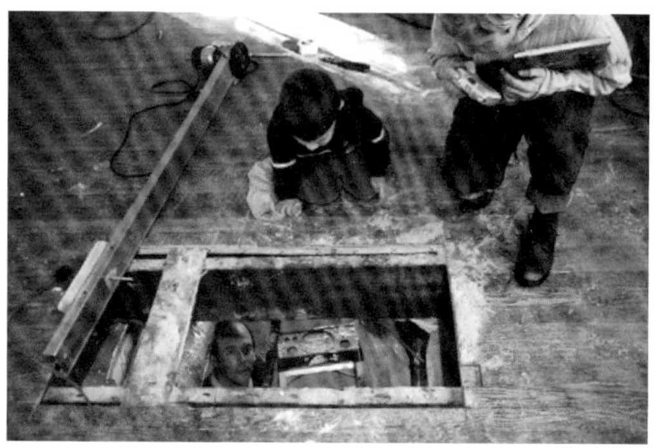

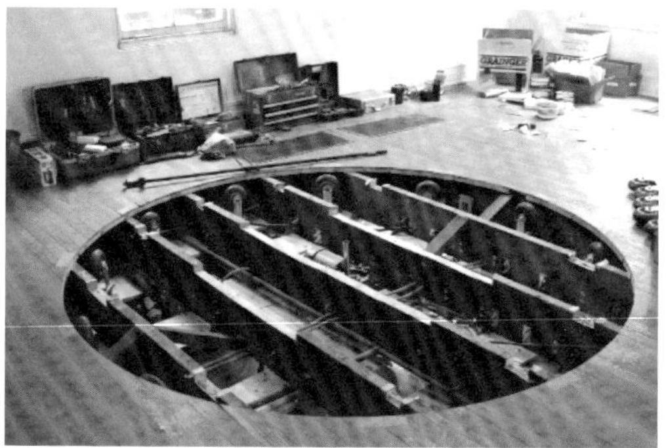

Ann Hamilton's installation *whitecloth* was conceived after a series of visits by the artist to The Aldrich Museum. She responded to the incongruity between the Museum's exterior appearance—an austere historic home—and its interior life as a changing exhibition space for contemporary art. This architectural dichotomy prompted Ann's ideas for an installation of sculpture responding to the building's unique architectural history.

The Aldrich is housed in a 1783 colonial structure once nicknamed "Old Hundred" for its community service from 1783 to 1883 as a general store, post office, and town meeting place. In 1883 "Old Hundred" was remodeled as a private residence. In 1929 it became the First Church of Christ, Scientist and in 1964 the building was purchased by Larry Aldrich and converted into a museum for contemporary art.

Hamilton initiated *whitecloth* by revealing thirteen windows which had been covered over during the 1964 conversion. The space, animated by the return of natural light and a view to the exterior, again became the context for domestic objects transformed by movement and touch. Some pieces are imbedded into the building's membrane, some cut through walls and pass through floors, others are arranged in the space like objects in a still life.

The process of responding to the building and its social history was accompanied and shaped by frequent conversations between Hamilton and poet Ann Lauterbach. The conversations, which focused on the written and vocalized word in early New England culture, generated ideas and themes which take shape in *whitecloth*. These themes also materialize in Lauterbach's poem, *All View (13 Windows)*, and are further elucidated in Nancy Princenthal's essay.

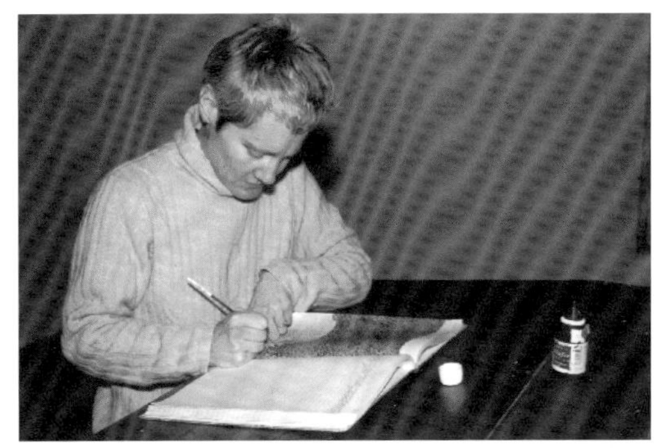

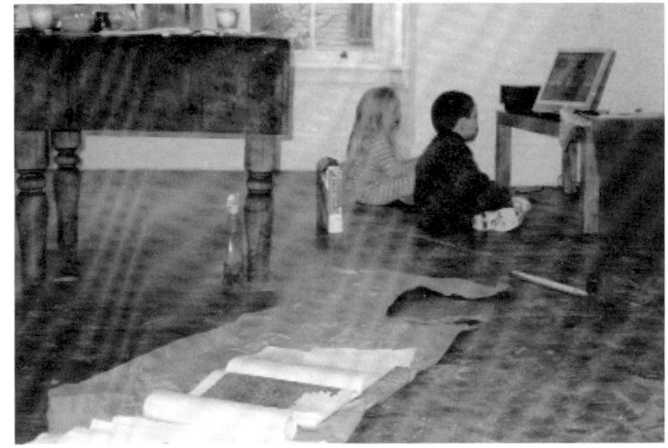

All of the photographs in the catalogue are views of *whitecloth* installed at The Aldrich Museum with the following exceptions: the image on page 4 was taken in the artist's studio; the photographs on pages 10 through 34 are of the windows which were exposed as part of the installation; the image on page 44 is a still from the video set in the wall near the butcher block table seen on page 42; the images on page 51 are stills from the video that is set into the desk visible in the foreground of the photograph on page 50; the sketches on the end papers are preparatory drawings for the layout of *whitecloth* by Hamilton.

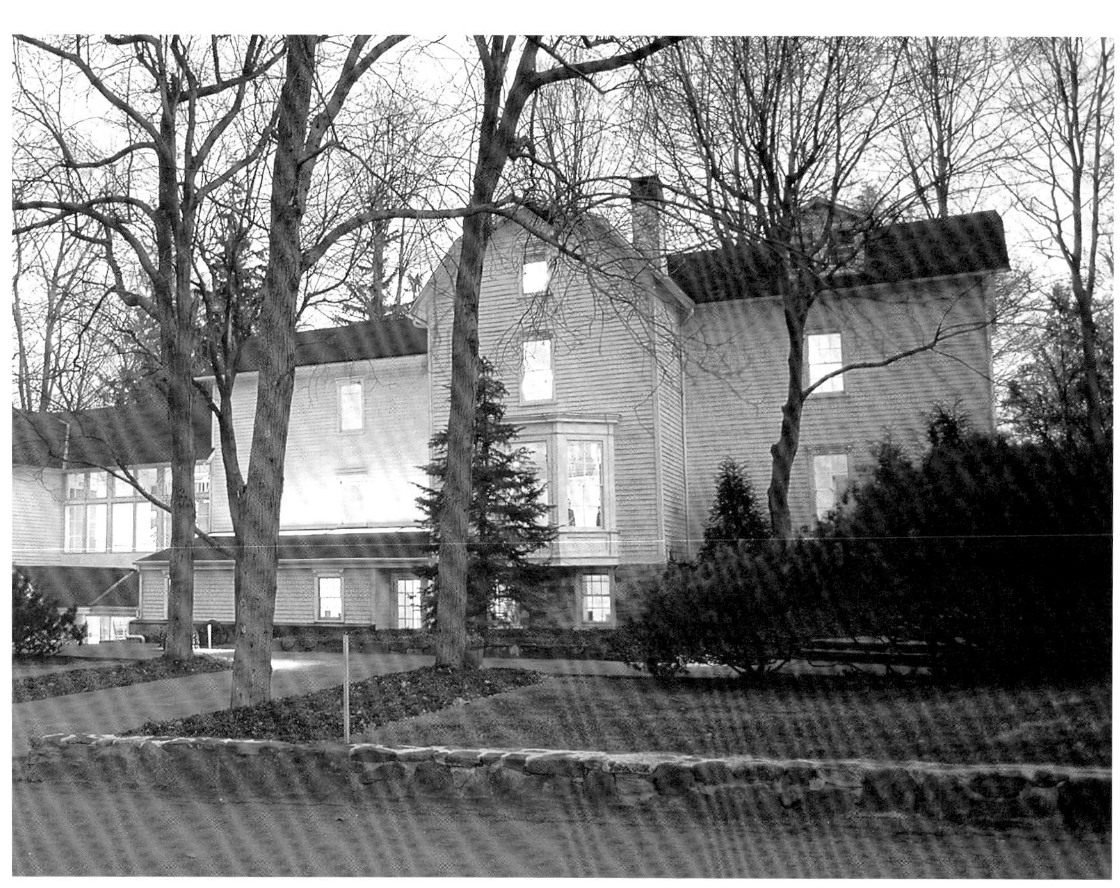

ALL VIEW (13 WINDOWS)

Ann Lauterbach

"the moral fact of the Unattainable, the flying Perfect"

—Emerson

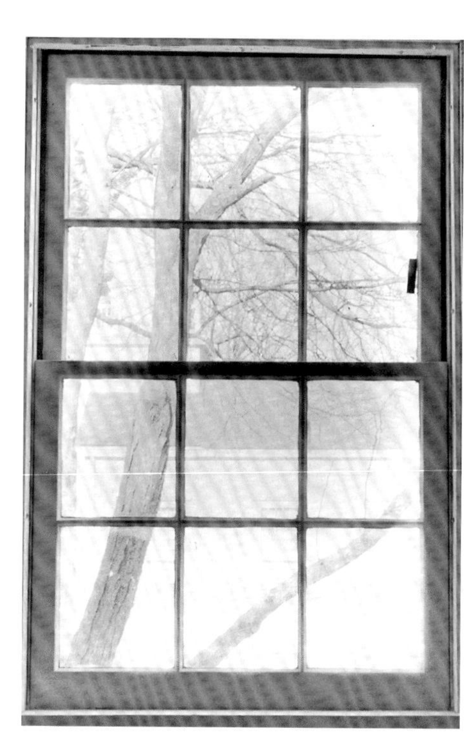

And here unfold Whitecloth

window

N

widow

comes loose initial animates

first habits shade

hemstitched into Name

adrift on grass/glass corona of breath waves

dewy weeds in air

And here untold

beyond our eyes a portrait

witness/absorb

where the fluid mirror weaves

terrains of hope into time's material covenant

birds sling webs in air

and the bewitched breath, its

fleet endurance, guides

tablet to light, light to

page inscribes/exhales

inundated spectral

an Invisible real

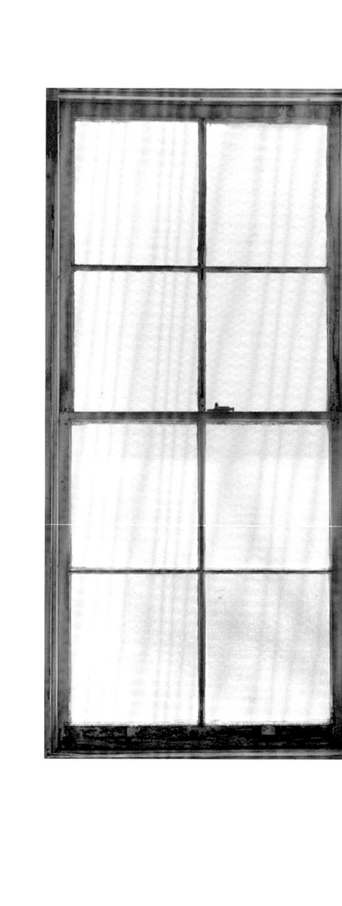

And so be held   in suspense

sweet Flag floats up

speculative   field into field   American   (*nugget nugget*)

seed of   *A*   *A*

A b r a h a m

f r o m   *C*

t o   *s h*   *i n*   *i*   *n*   *g*

holds a lens   lends a hand

surrounds

back through the stitched loop

the ghost hole

calls the Body into its House

but who can say who I am

through this

open

hand/eye/mouth?

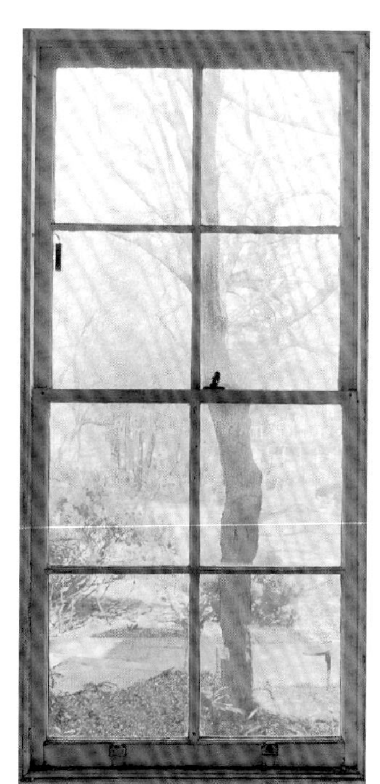

Light's cowl

dilates the span
found in the grave elaborations
of the said

O

say

pattern of silhouette, cloud I d i d I d i d I d i d

I think, Mr. Williams, I must now confess to you, that the most wise God hath provided and cut out this part of the world for a refuge and a receptacle for all sorts of consciences. I am now under a cloud, and my brother Hooker, with the Bay, as you have been; we have removed from them thus far, and yet they are not satisfied.

filmed over the yard's spire

spindle, rod

cast upon water
unsheltered synecdoche of touch

over the local Commons
grave grass

pinwheel/windmill
through the spun

leafy redundancy
global swirl

tear in Whole Cloth

lexicon of embodied doubt

Mistress Anne *cast out as unsavory salt*

and so wears the itinerant grain

of the vagrant, wind

of the unannounced, details yet to come, drop by drop

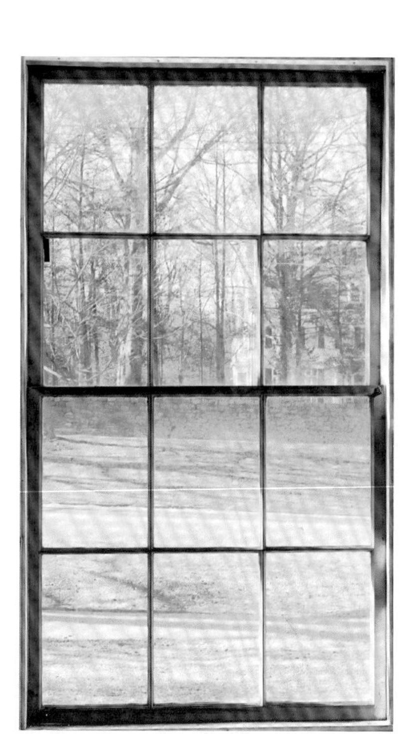

To bleed Wilderness   is strange

untell the story

open the plan the palm   (map)

attempt   a t i o   n a t i o n s t a t   i o n

T

cast off initial Time   preempt/impede

I am a transparent clock

O say   we shall allow all   to see

wait   patient recess

for wee must Consider that wee shall be as a Citty upon a Hill
the eies of all people are uppun us.

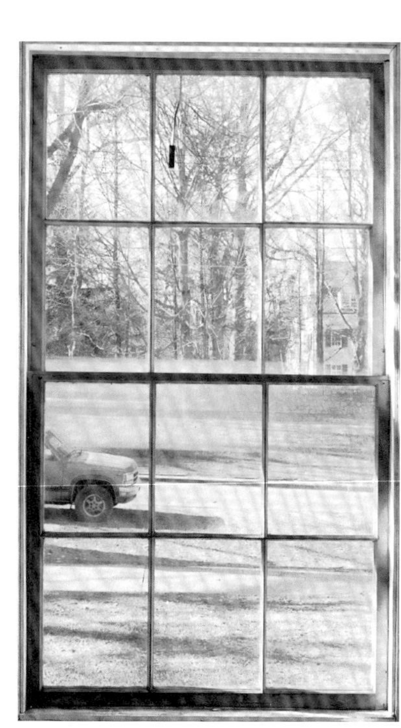

Re   store tore ore

Pastorale ease

E as E

aural   Err/or

Err/and

R R R

e r a s e   a r i s e

official coin   heads tails   incident   Fundamental Orders

chance or fate

rapacious rerun
night narrates Progress

cold resuscitation of the norm   breaks her fast
Whitecloth spread over the enormous table

spoon   plate   cup

deserted alcove

that the sojourn iterates   sun
into the empty grove

go up over the ravine   ray vine
into the blossoms of dawn

count backwards past   Z   rose/Eros   into the sky's plural One

minute breath intact

and the mobile need
saturates the glistening Cloth

pocket of heavy tears

locket of stars

Who set those candles, those torches of heaven, on the table? Who hung out those lanterns in heaven to enlighten a dark world?

—Thomas Shepard

Ah! Dainty—dainty Death! Ah! democratic Death! Grasping the proudest zinnia from my purple garden,—then deep to his bosom calling the serf's child!

Say, is he everywhere? Where shall I hide my things? Who is alive? The woods are dead. Is Mrs. H. alive? Annie and Katie—are they below, or received to nowhere?

I shall not tell how short time is, for I was told by lips which sealed as soon as it was said, and the open revere the shut. You were not here in summer. Summer? My memory flutters—had I—was there a summer? You should have seen the fields go—gay little entomology! Swift little ornithology! Dancer, and floor, and cadence quite gathered away, and I, a phantom, to you a phantom, rehearse the story! An orator of feather unto an audience of fuzz,—and pantomimic plaudits.

—Emily Dickinson

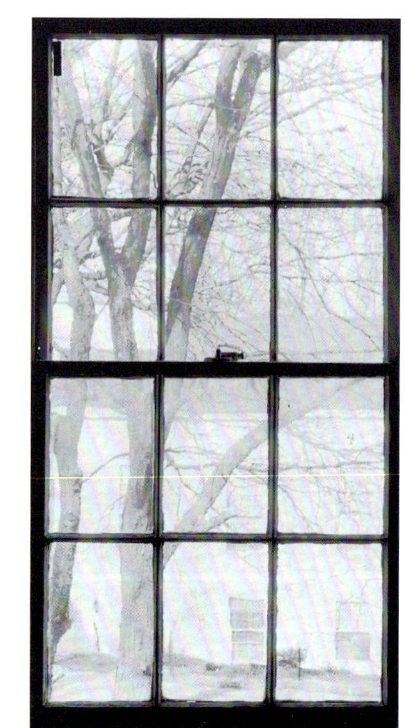

Herald

mouth's pale diction   elemental alphabet

suspended over the hot noise

doctrine of belief, thought's melancholy stitch, its harbor shifting overhead, deed anchored

in the Valley

inhale

parched Pilgrim these remnants

get thee hence

unsettle usher into our path   convert

the sense of the heart

Harvest

letter by letter

f l e e c e   o f   t h e   b l a c k   s h e e p

V e i l   o f   t h e   B r i d e

your true script

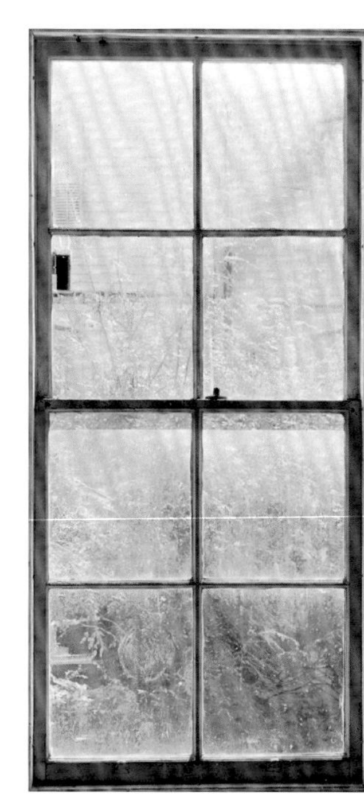

. . . I have seen vast multitudes of little shining webs and glistening strings, brightly reflecting the sunbeams, and some of them of a great length, and at such a height that one would think that they were tacked to the vault of the heavens, and would be burnt like tow in the sun, . . .

filled flame   Salvation Bride   alcove   Love's stamp

Let her

match
ringed Fate

in the blink of an eye   *shutter fact*   *I do*

cyclic nerve whose journey disassembles the cogent object
mechanical warp and the hooped gesticulations of arrival
as the ink becomes manifest

the life of things the blind Cloth raised

aperture   rapture   capture

parade on Main Street
welcome bells
alert in the rood tower   flag
billowing out drums pounding

the great announcement
the evident proof

Observe

worthy Scientist   quest and profit   event and thing

each Spider's horizon

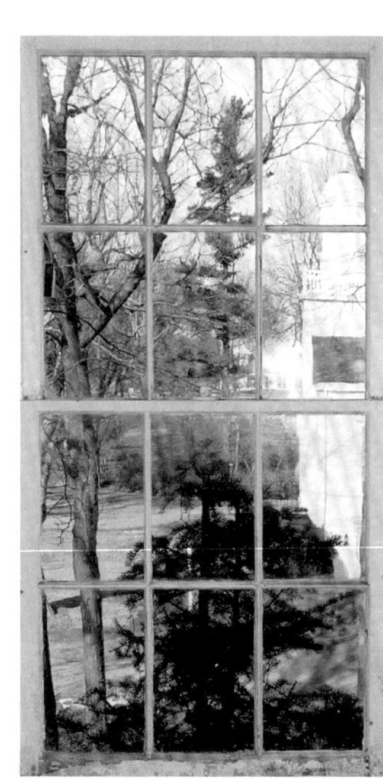

And the desolate champion of noon, the wide roof bruised with copper and shale, bright motif of solid fire that the preacher had preached, and who am I to say what you saw, peeling the architecture back to its original fabric, the cot by the door, the small blooms in their pewter vase, the stolid floor furbished to a gleam ——

saw as the winter sky
wheeled through its paces
the sudden luminous set

violence
quickening to the west

whitest of whites
splashed onto the twigs' icy script

these weathers ——

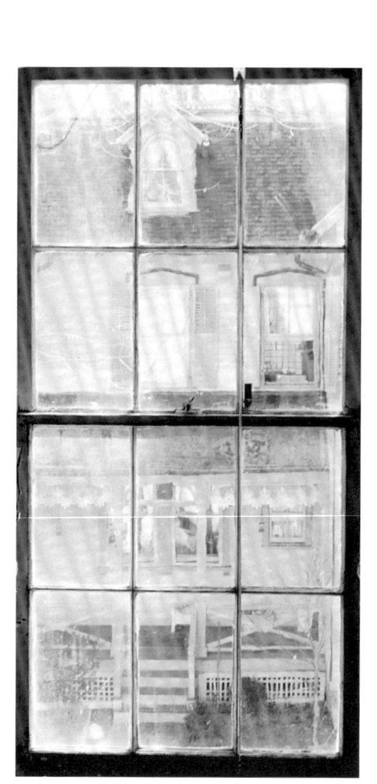

These instruments
here to touch an ordinary

hearth
gazing out from the domestic pond

whose world
converts into a mirror breathing

into the predilection to rise
easily from the ghost-strewn crib

out of the night shade
into the Book ——

ecstatic sheet
beyond such boundaries of the given

beyond the kitchen sink ——
into Jerusalem

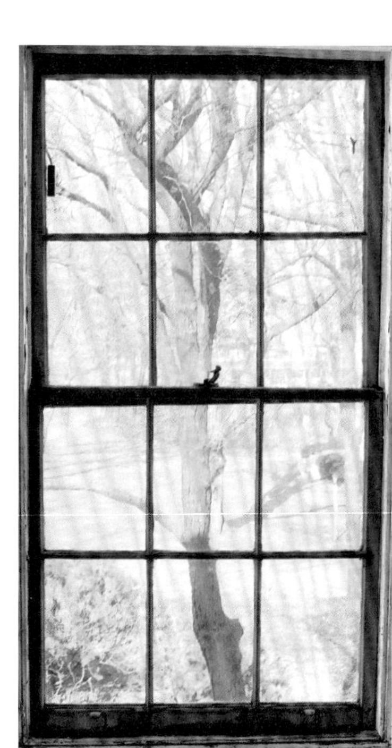

Her oath

teller told her oath
to safely keep (beyond bondage) yes

attendance

and the loose ribbons in her hair
and the garment at her feet

and then went down

to kiss

anointed thus mouth to mouth halo or mark

to conceive Evening's branch

Staff

(to not forsake)

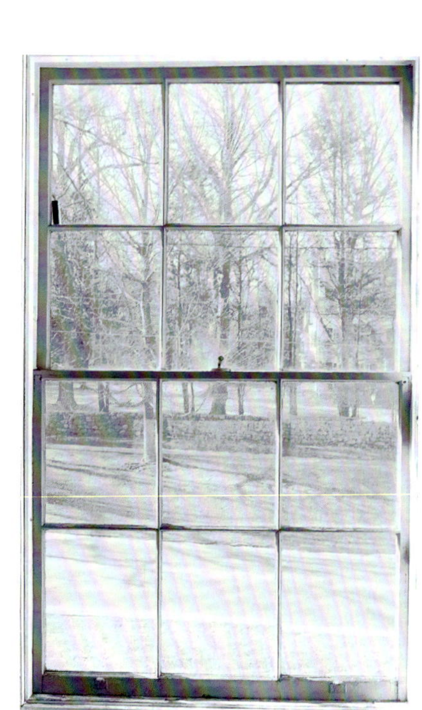

So that we might revisit the cabinet of Hours, where the stamps are, where the Bees
concoct their slow cascading wealth, where the testimonies come forth from the fingers'
blue alphabet, the neck severed from its body, the body
cannot sing
without shattering
through etymologies of purpose

figura

praised into Sound

the shape of grace

and the wall sweats
and the route the Cloth takes

through the arc

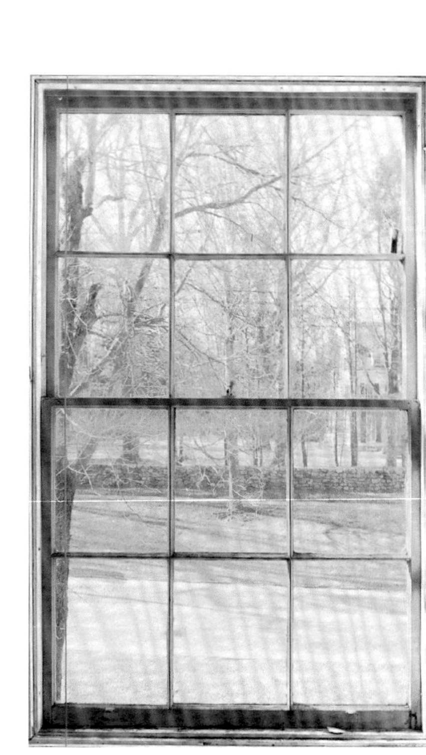

To retrieve Newness

to find

Original Sound

in the wound of the ear

Abide empirical fact

and the naked Apparition
skirting these thresholds

into the Space where nothing always is
about to be

Whitecloth

lifts angle of sun across her face

caps breaking

sail set

rim

Museum

and toy boat

Ann Hamilton: *whitecloth*

Nancy Princenthal

The slightly tattered, square white cloth moves overhead ceaselessly but unpredictably, its indirect forward progress interrupted by short, vigorous reversals, its speed the hand-operated tempo of laundry being hauled in—impatiently, gladly, in anger, in grace. It travels (on a motor-driven wire, regulated by a computer-governed 64,000-move pattern of advances and retreats) from room to room and floor to floor, passing with a modest flutter in front of windows, slipping effortlessly through walls and floors, and whisking out of sight into the attic before returning to the light-filled, domestic rooms below. As if transported by a slightly giddy sleepwalker, or ghost, the cloth advances trancelike and heedless of obstacles. It is, portentously, a first signal of a body's absence. But viewers who wish to follow its passage without interruption will find themselves dashing indecorously for stairways and halls, only too aware of obtuse physicality. (Observant visitors will discover, in so doing, that the apparently single cloth is not one but two, traveling the same route but widely separated.) Evocative of a maiden's veil, a gentleman's handkerchief, and the white scarf pulled out of a magician's sleeve, the white cloth is a sign of surrender in war or, by

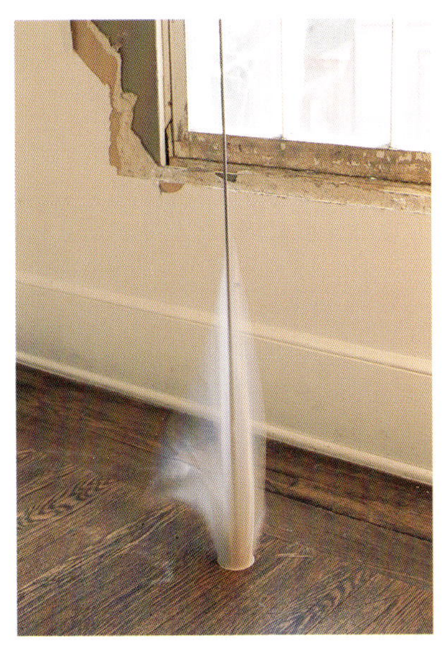
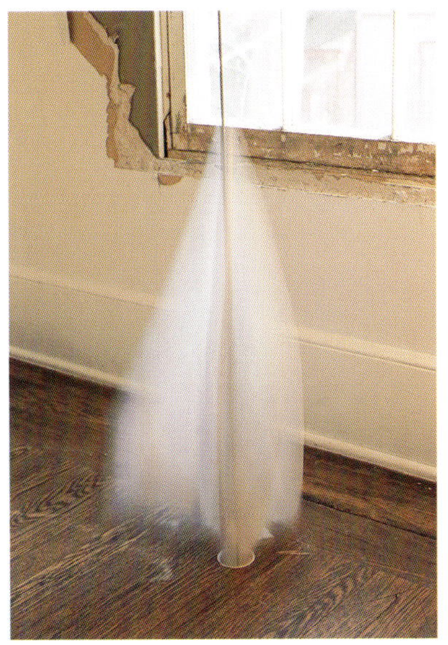
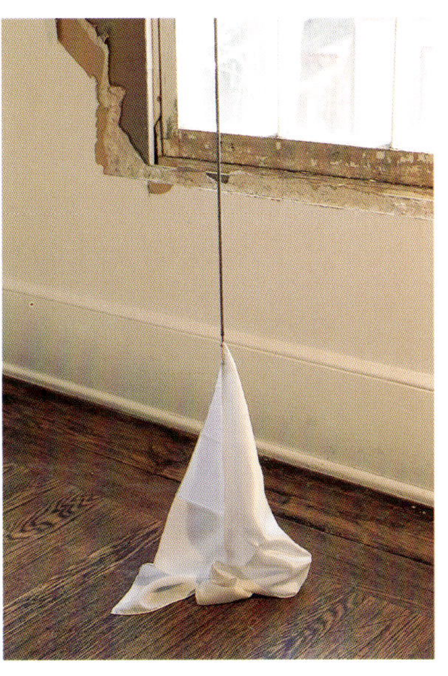
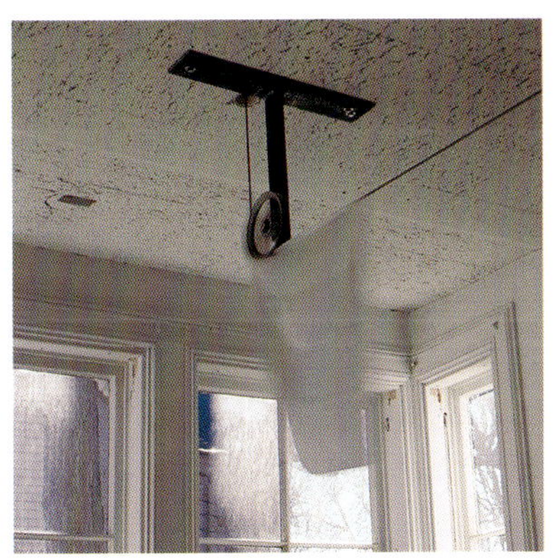
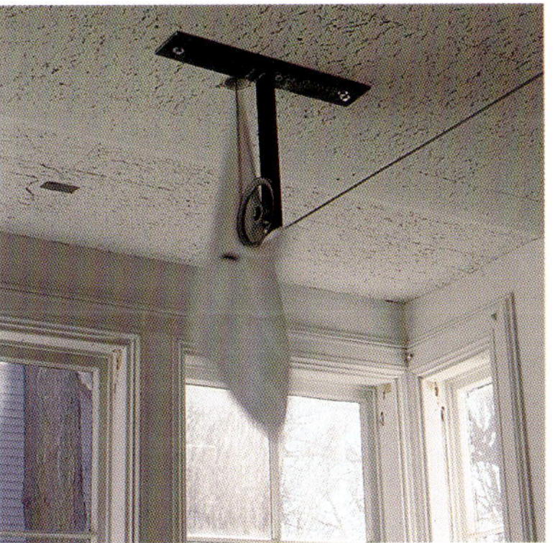
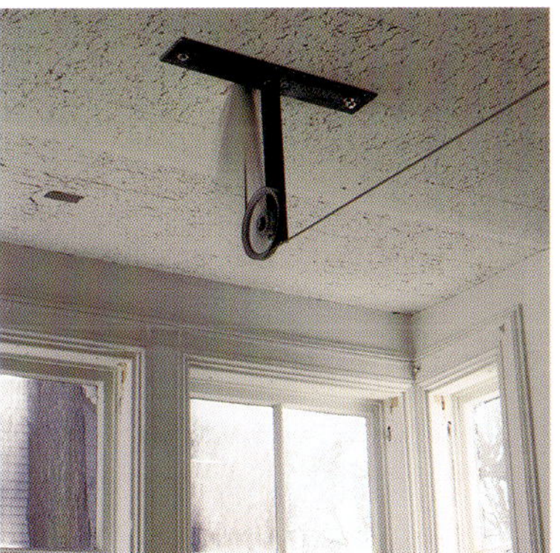

Victorian cliché, in love. A symbol of spotless purity, it can be made to perform, as here, like a shameless tease. Associated with rituals of both birth and death, it is, in Christian religious imagery, a receptacle for miraculous impressions: the Shroud of Turin, Veronica's Veil. In secular material culture, on the other hand, the white cloth is a metonym for every painting ever painted on a blank white canvas. As the titular subject for Ann Hamilton's museum-wide installation at The Aldrich Museum, the white cloth is, in short, an abundantly symbolic form that runs through the exhibition in more ways than one.

Hamilton was trained in weaving and textile design (at the University of Kansas; she also earned a Master of Fine Arts in sculpture at Yale), and has used cloth in many previous exhibitions. "My first hand," she has said, "is a sewing hand."[1] Most recently, in *mattering* (created for the Musée d'art Contemporain at Lyons, 1997), an enormous expanse of orange silk billowed overhead; visitors shared the luminous, tented space with a flock of peacocks. *bounden*, created for the same exhibition, involved enormous curtains embroidered with text. There have been tables piled with cloth, and walls lined with it. In *filament*, as seen at the Sean Kelly Gallery in 1996, a circular curtain, swirling like the skirt of a fevered dancer blocked the entryway. Suspended cloth also shaped viewers' passage through *mneme* (Tate Gallery, Liverpool, 1994). One of the most venerable of artifacts (it is older than pottery by more than a millenium), cloth, when reduced to animal fiber—as in the horsehair carpet of *tropos* (Dia, 1993)—appears at an intersection of particular interest to Hamilton: that between human and animal. Equally appealing to Hamilton is its position at another fundamental threshold: "Like human skin," she has said, cloth "is a membrane that divides an interior from an exterior. It both reveals and conceals."[2]

At The Aldrich, another white cloth plays a leading role, in which it is made to levitate above a refectory-sized wooden table. The unembellished, satiny tablecloth billows lustily a few inches above the tabletop, held aloft by jets of air that are channeled through the table's legs before issuing from minute holes in its surface; the cloth is discreetly tethered to the table by tiny threads. References are, again, manifold, chief among them the séances and other spiritualist exercises popular in the late nineteenth century, and also Christian observances: the Last Supper and its prefiguration of death; the communion table, and the cycle of sacrifice and rebirth, material ingestion and spiritual sustenance enacted in the sacrament of the Eucharist. Writhing and rippling above the unseen jets of air, the cloth also unmistakably suggests the sheet of a conjugal bed, filling out the same family of associations—with purity, sensuality, and mortality—evoked by the circulating white cloth. Tables, too are a feature of much of Hamilton's previous work, and elsewhere in *whitecloth*, they appear several times, notably in the form of a double-length butcher-block table, which Hamilton is displaying as she found it, marked by decades of use and redolent of both manual labor and animal flesh. Considered in the broadest terms, the table figures prominently in several influential theoretical frameworks for postwar art, from Leo Steinberg's 1972 essay

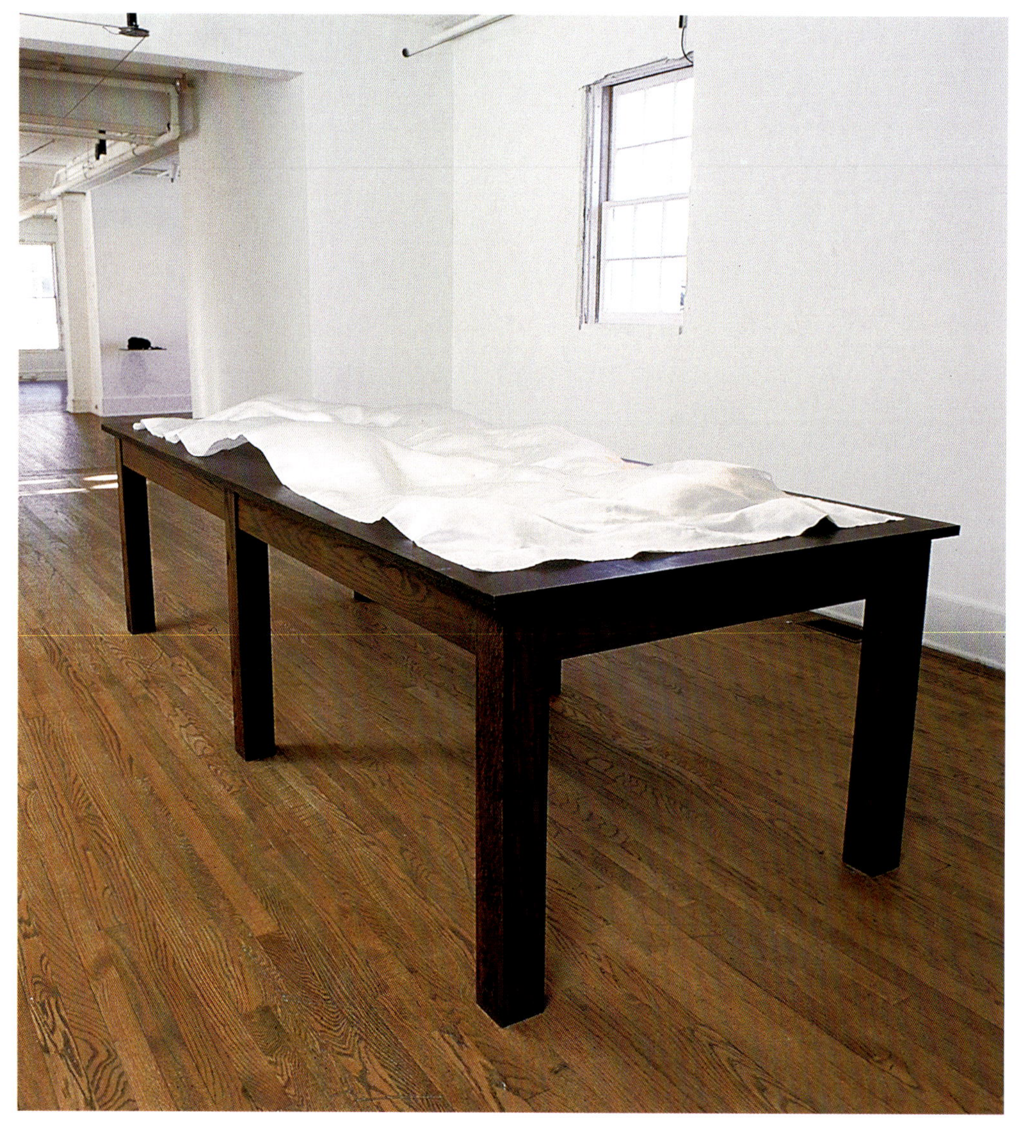

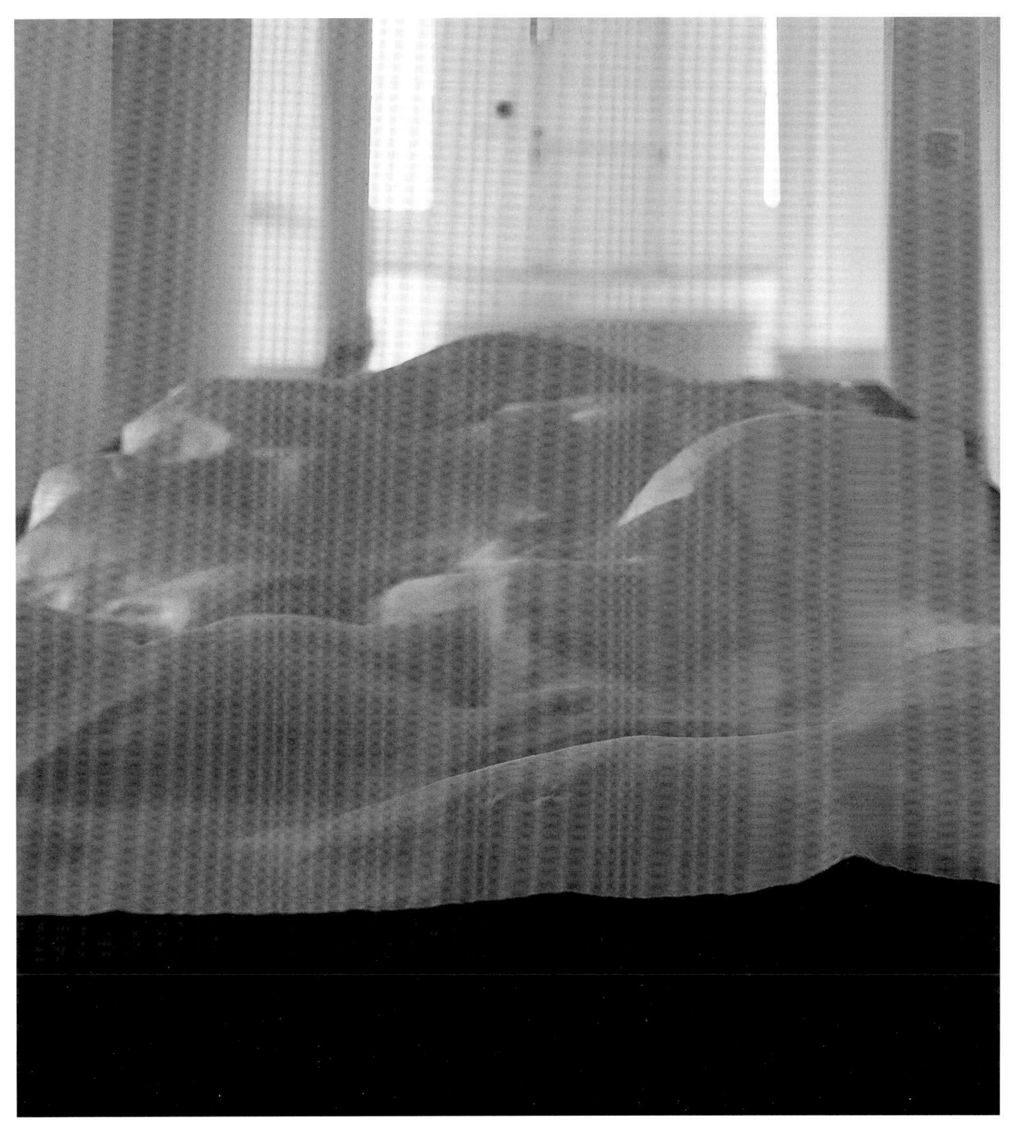

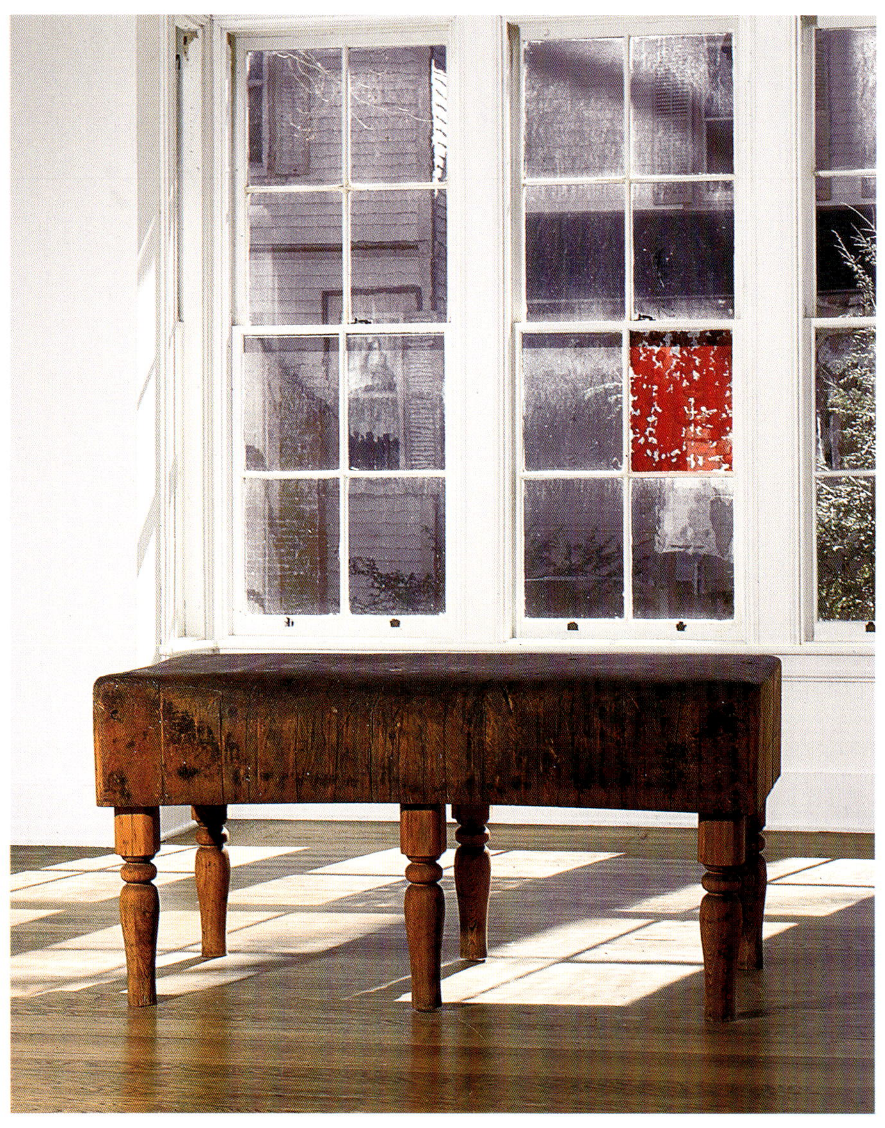

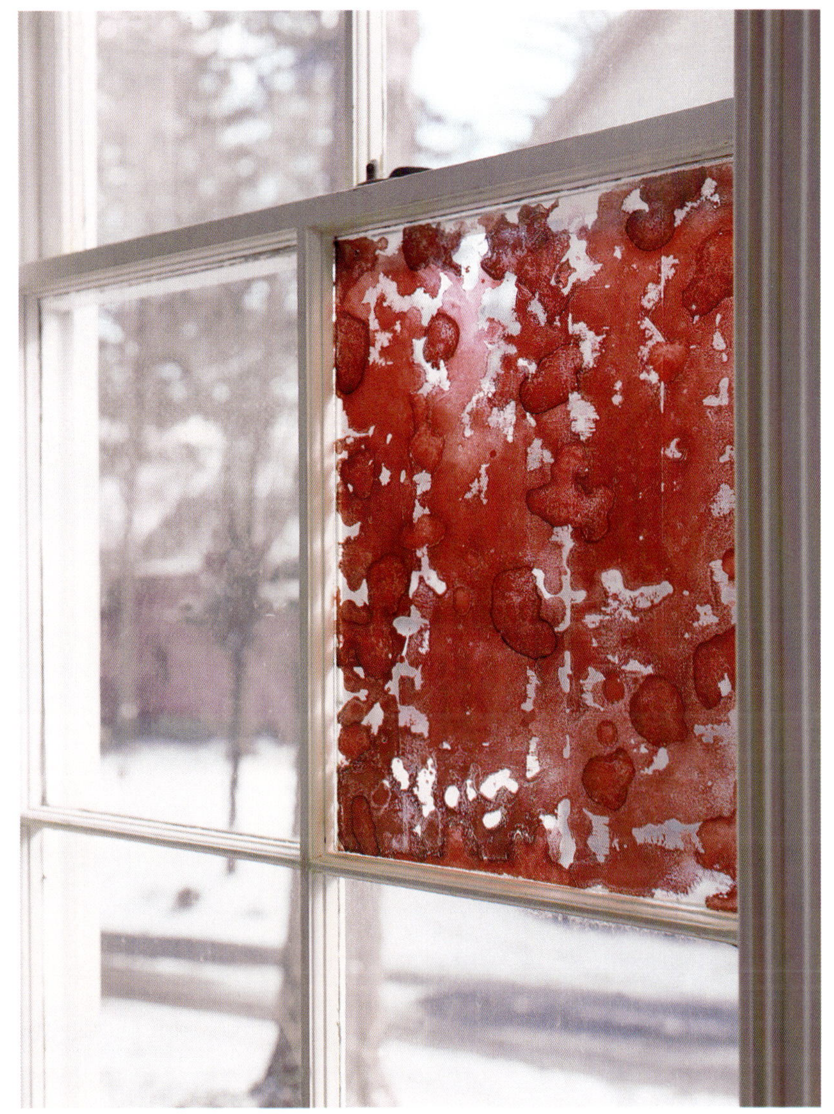

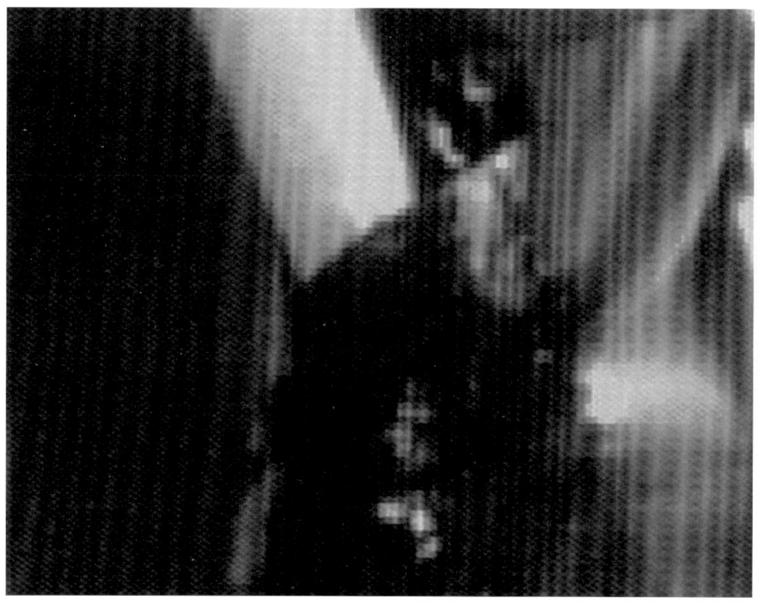

nominating the "flatbed" surface, with its horizontal orientation, as prototypical for a new understanding of art's literal, information-bearing status,[3] to Philip Fisher's recent discussion (in a book much admired by Hamilton) of the table as a paradigmatic crafted object, product of unalienated labor and, until modernism, model of the art object. "The table," Fisher writes, "was uniquely adjusted to the radius of the human will."[4]

But in her use of tables, as throughout the exhibition, Hamilton is less interested in broad theoretical accounts of contemporary art than specific narratives of particular venues. At The Aldrich, she was afforded a remarkably long and full history. The portion of the current Museum in which *whitecloth* is installed[5] was built in 1783 by two lieutenants in the Revolutionary War, and began its life as that quintessential American institution, the general store. Offering hardware, dry goods, and a local meeting place, the building also served—typically for the time—as a post office, establishing an early and enduring link between commerce and communication. A hundred years later, the building was converted to a residence, the home of Grace King Ingersoll, a descendant of one of its builders. In 1929, a fateful year in American socioeconomics, the structure was converted to a house of worship, becoming Ridgefield's First Church of Christ, Scientist. Finally, in 1964, amid a flourishing economy and burgeoning American art world, contemporary art collector Larry Aldrich remodeled the church as a museum.

Christian Science, founded by Mary Baker Eddy in 1866, is in many ways a representative expression of late nineteenth-century New England culture, proposing as it does a resolution of materialistic science and religious faith. Eddy, a New Englander much influenced by Emerson's transcendentalism, was especially leery of medicine's inroads into mortality's border zones. She conceived of Christ as a supreme physician, science as an attribute of the divine Mind, and matter as utterly negligible. "My first plank in the platform of Christian Science is as follows," she wrote. "There is no life, truth, intelligence, nor substance in matter. All is infinite Mind and its infinite manifestation, for God is All-in-all." Moreover, true faith has observable consequence, for, Eddy wrote, "it wrought my immediate recovery from an injury caused by an

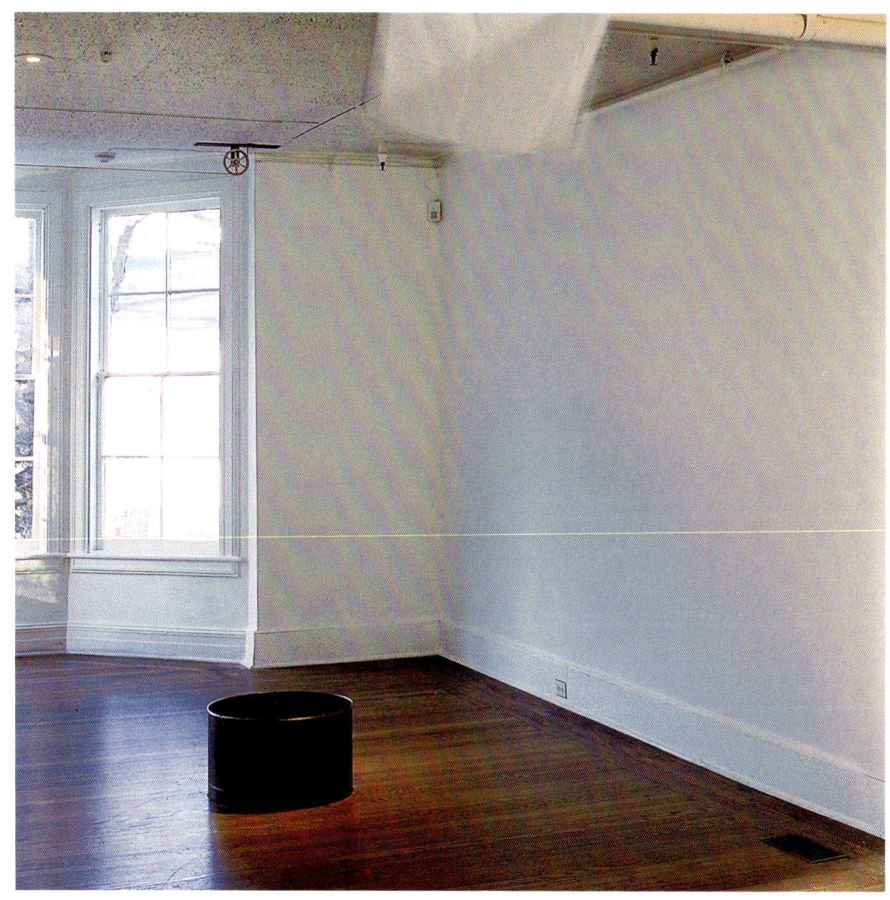

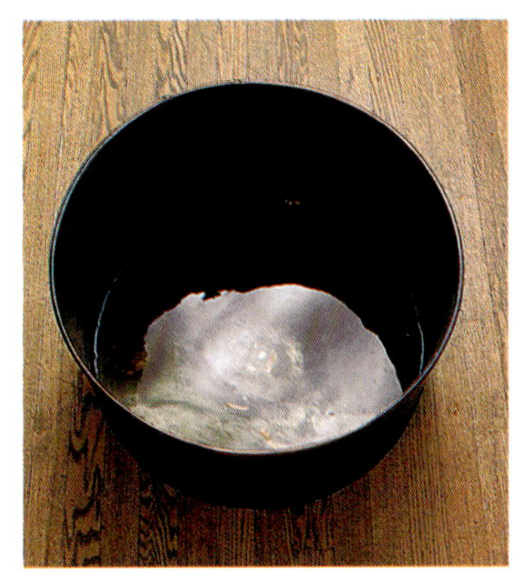

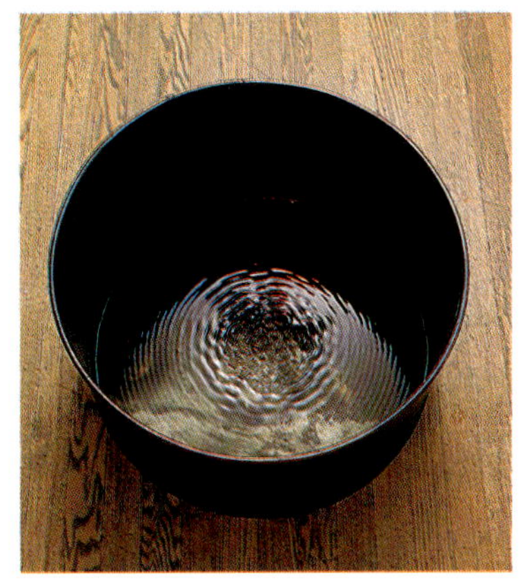

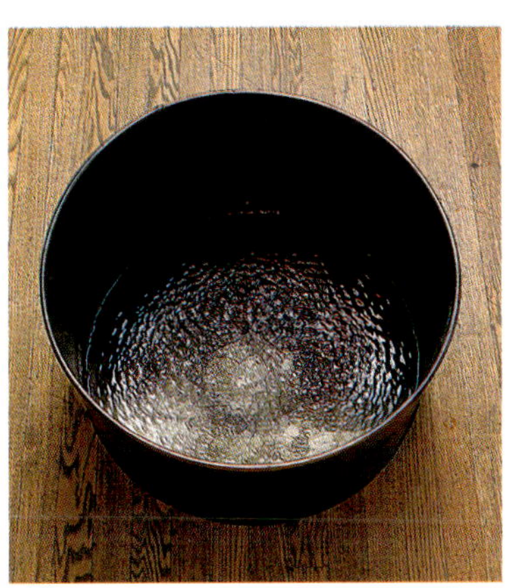

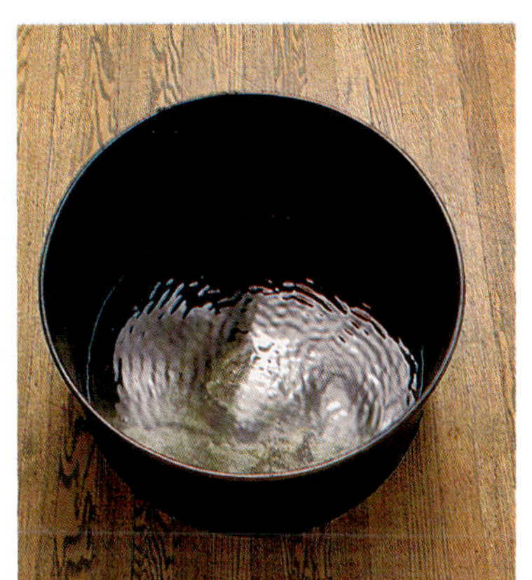

accident, and pronounced fatal by the physicians." What might have been called hysterical illness (especially as its spontaneously recovering victim was a woman) was instead taken as evidence of divine power, and piety rewarded.

That a contest over faith should take place on the field of the (female) body is of great interest to Hamilton, and made more so by being staged against a domestic backdrop. The constellation of issues presented by The Aldrich's history—the New England dowager's house consecrated as a church founded by a woman; the legacy, so strong locally, of Puritanism with its emphasis on devotion and denial of the flesh; and, not least, the series of

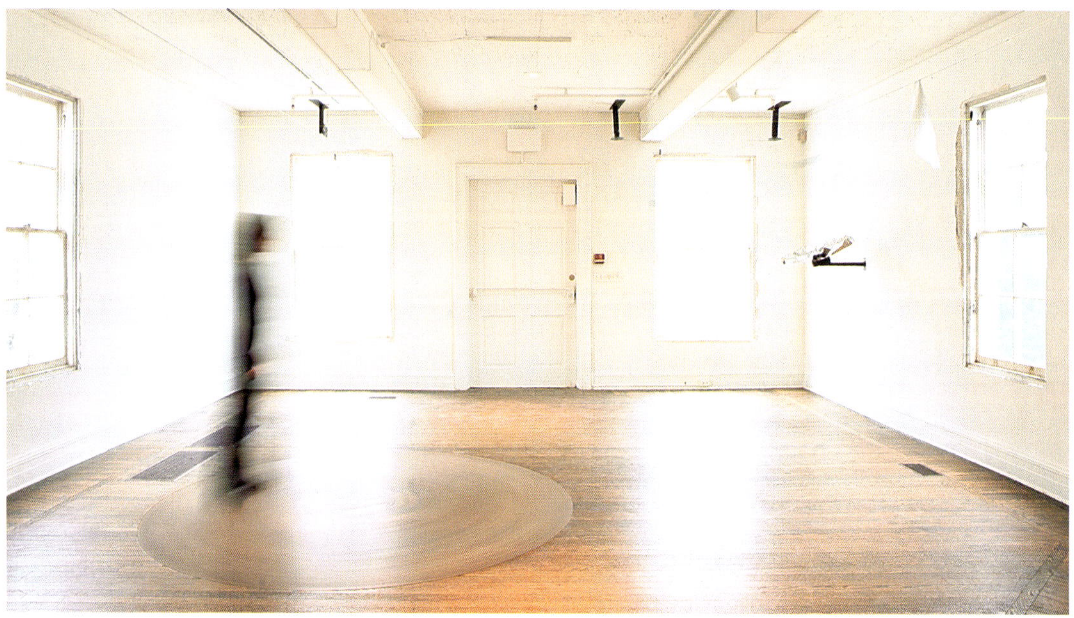

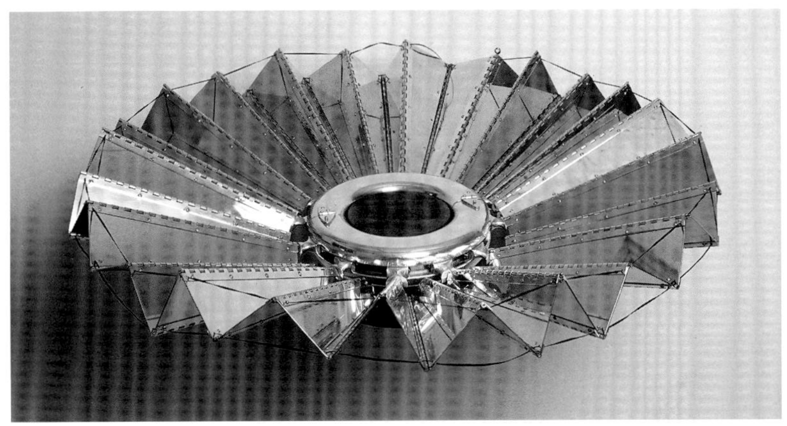

historical accidents by which these stories all came to be layered over each other in this stately white clapboard building—are all remarkably consonant with Hamilton's longstanding interests. Research for *whitecloth* led her to explore the intellectual history of colonial New England, and particularly the seventeenth century antinomian controversy involving Massachusetts Bay colonist Anne Hutchinson. In the mid-1630s, Hutchinson, prompted by spiritual inspiration, urged followers to seek and embrace divine grace directly; the schismatic practice was called antinomianism. As described by poet Susan Howe (in a book of essays favored by Hamilton), "An antinomian is a religious enthusiast. Noah Webster defines an enthusiast as '1. One who imagines he has special or supernatural converse with God, or special communications from him. 2. One whose imagination is warmed . . . '"[6] Hutchinson's beliefs were found to be in direct contradiction to the strict

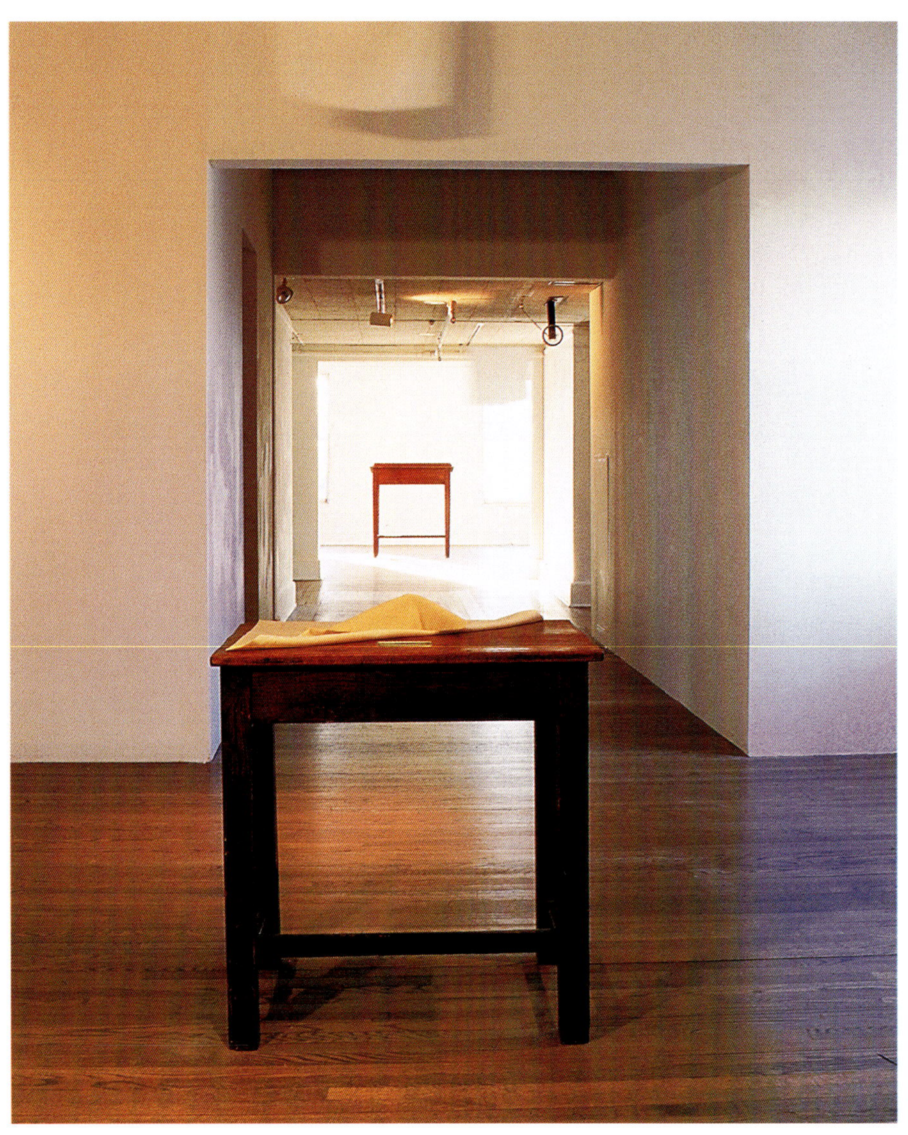

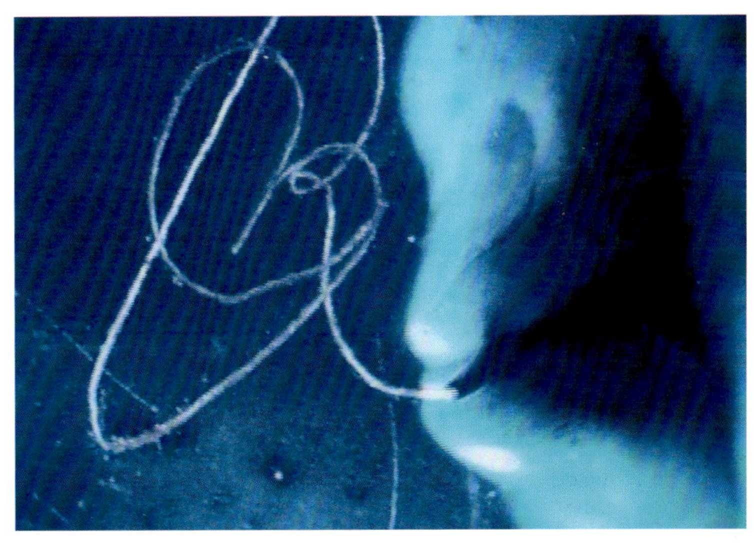

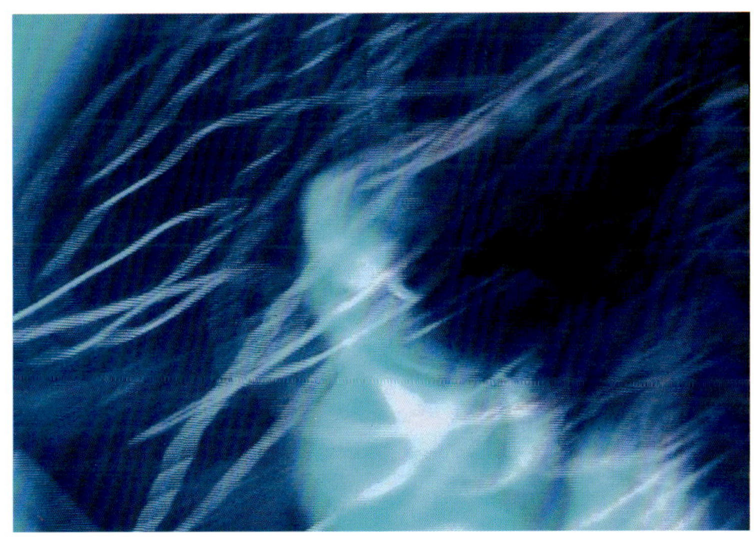

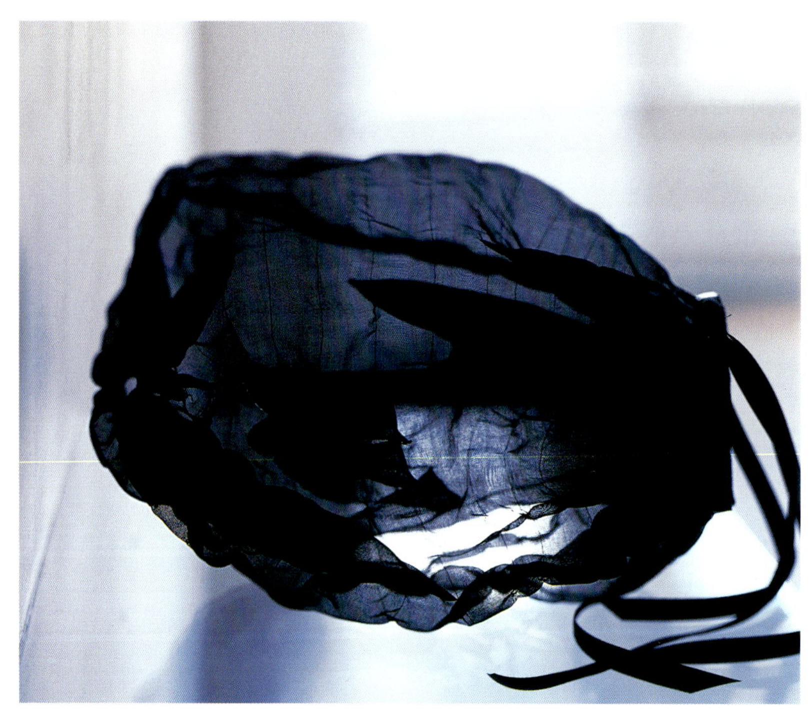

Calvinism of the colony's Puritan leaders, who preached the futility of trusting intuitive experience of Divine pleasure; indeed self-conscious physical experience—and pleasure of any kind—were considered indicative of grievous lapses in faith. As Howe relates, Hutchinson was lectured in court (before being banished from the colony), condemned for unwomanly insubordination as much as heresy: "you have stept out of your place, you *have rather bine a Husband than a Wife and a preacher than a Hearer; and a Magistrate than a Subject*. And soe you have thought to carry all Thinges in Church and Commonwealth, as you would and have not bine humbled for this."[7]

The schism between those who—following a powerful, ardent woman—advocated immediate acceptance of divine grace, and those who insisted that it be either contingent on good works or preordained and unverifiable on earth, offers a rich historical metaphor for the opposition between subjective experience and its external register which runs throughout Hamilton's work. "The work has had so much to do with a border between an inside and an outside—between feeling and articulation, or the skin as something that contains but that also makes you a container," she has said[8] (the statement is closely related to her description of cloth). In *whitecloth*, the primary surrogate for the human body is the building itself. The very first thing that struck Hamilton about The Aldrich was "the tension between the building's exterior, which projects one thing, and its interior, which denies it."[9] As part of the conversion of the eighteenth-century structure to a twentieth-century museum, properly consisting of unadorned, rectilinear white galleries, thirteen windows had been concealed. Many other domestic (and ecclesiastic) details were similarly removed or concealed, notably fireplaces. From the outside, the alterations were not apparent, and the façade of domesticity was preserved. Hamilton's first and most basic expression of this architectural dissimulation was the removal of the drywall covering the windows. The rough edges of the torn walls and, in places, the coarse threads of the fabric that lined them were left exposed, suggesting, to Hamilton, a crude "surgical incision."[10] Inside, the ceiling—long black—was painted white.

Philip Fisher argues that the hallmark of twentieth century art is its anticipation, in its very conception, of the position it will occupy in the linear cultural history represented by the major art museums.[11] To apply Fisher's terms, Hamilton's act of dismantling illuminates the history while subverting the presumption of linear progress. By redirecting attention to the domestic and religious realms, she points art back toward the very contexts in which it had, each in turn, found intellectual and material support. Her complementary use of windows (venerable symbols, in pre-Modernist painting, of pictorial transparency to its subject) and of blank white cloth (which, conversely, stands for Modernist self-reflection, from Malevich to Ryman) can be seen as consistent with the polite violence she does to the protocols of "white cube" Modernist exhibition practice. There are connections, in this respect, to other recent artists' work, from Gordon Matta-Clark's famous acts of architectural rupture (chain-sawing giant freehand openings in walls and floors of abandoned buildings, shooting out the windows of an exhibition space) to Mona Hatoum's leisurely, fiber-optic photographic excursion from the skin of her own body to its interior.

But, again, the field in which *whitecloth* takes shape is more usefully defined by local history, and by the artist's own previous work. For instance, the inclination to fold history back on itself, treating it as a reversible narrative, is related to Hamilton's frequent use of erasure, usually not to do with undoing architecture but with effacing text, by burning lines of print with a heated stylus, or rubbing them out with spit, or obscuring them with pebbles.[12] In *whitecloth*, this impulse can be seen in several works involving writing; like all of the major freestanding elements in the show, they are each paired with a newly revealed window. One consists of a lectern, into the top of which a window was cut and fitted with glass that is in turn covered by a liturgical-looking cream-colored cloth. Beneath is an old-fashioned ledger in which Hamilton wrote out the text of a sermon by famous Puritan minister and historian Cotton Mather, grandson of one of Anne Hutchinson's most prominent adversaries. The sermon is copied in a careful cursive script that looks childishly labored, but is actually quite demonically rampant: words are connected end to end, and the loops of letters touch top to bottom on succeeding lines, forming a dense, nearly unreadable linear fabric that was made still more impenetrable by Hamilton's having painstakingly filled the spaces between each penstroke with blood-red ink. This self-devouring script is also, paradoxically, an almost literal image of the word made flesh; the latter reference is picked up in an alteration of a window downstairs, in which an existing pane of glass was replaced with

The Text is Like the Cloudy and Fiery Pillar, vouchsafed unto *Israel*, in the Wilderness of old; there is a very *dark side* of it in the Intimation, that, *The Devil is come down having great Wrath*; but it has also a *bright side*, when it assures us, that *He has but a short time*; Unto the Contemplation of *both*, I do this Day Invite you.

From Cotton Mather, "A Discourse on the Wonders of the Invisible World."

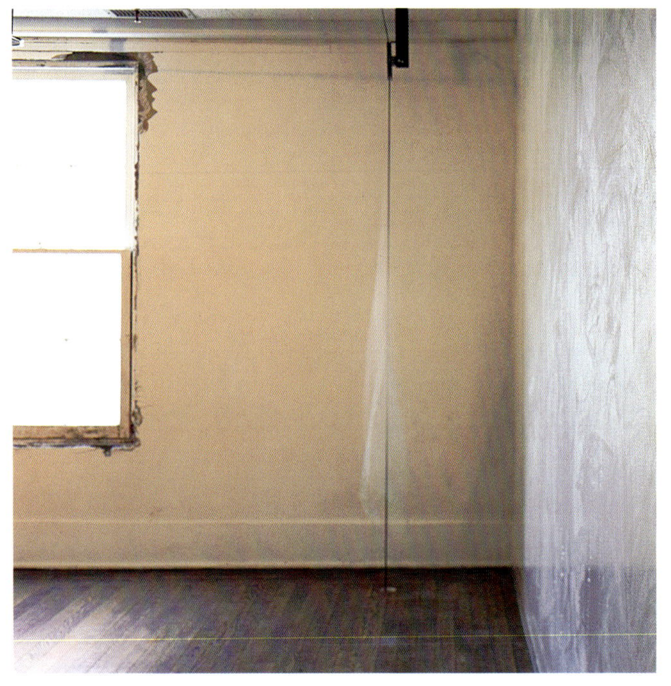

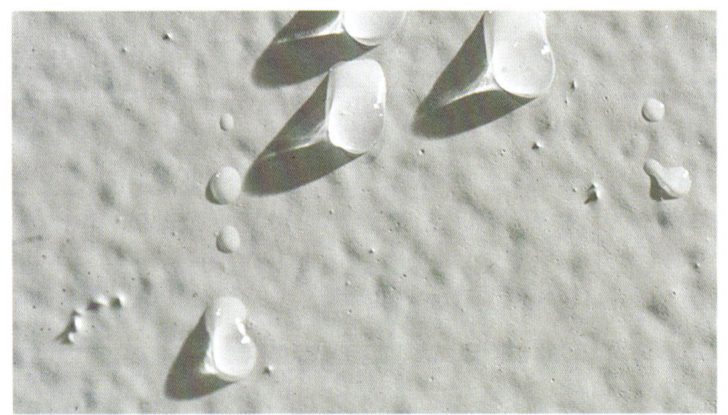

one stained in pooling layers of the same red ink. The connection with flesh has a further extension, as this is the window through which light is cast on the butcher-block table. That the red-inked windowpane at once suggests a microscope slide and Gothic stained glass is the kind of doubled meaning that Mather himself favored, in the form of anagrams and puns.

Wordplay interests Hamilton as well, as do many other ways language can be rendered opaque, from stressing its visual qualities to layering it with a degree of density that amounts—like speaking in tongues—to a kind of semantic ecstasy. In a videotape reinstalled for *whitecloth*,[13] a hand holding a stylus can be seen carefully inscribing the alphabet onto a pane of inked glass; again, the letters are run in, and also inverted (this monitor is set into the top of a small table, so the writing is seen backwards, from above), making them nearly impossible to decipher. This kind of deliberate but breathless writing evokes the mythically eternal needlework associated with figures of determined female resistance as far back as Penelope and Ariadne. In *whitecloth*, the connection between writing and sewing is made explicit in a book-shaped sculpture that houses a thimble into which has been cut, continuously and in negative, Susan Stewart's *Cinder*, a poem of surpassingly graceful circularity. The letter-to-letter interconnectedness of writing within the textual elements of *whitecloth* is paralleled in the web of symbolic links between them, and further in other works in the installation, though each seems at first utterly self-possessed and discrete. Following the lines they weave, in ever increasing proliferation, leads the viewer on an intellectual steeplechase that runs in tandem with the pursuit, through its unpredictable, unstoppable journey, of the circulating white cloth.

The description of the viewer as a kind of perceptual decathlon contestant is not altogether idle. Hamilton has often used live performers in her work, or represented the traces of their actions. In *whitecloth*, not for the first time, the viewer serves in some ways as the absent performer, operating various elements more or less literally. This invitation to active participation, or at least to acute physical self-consciousness, complements the invocation throughout the installation of an absent body. In addition to establishing patterns of viewing that superimpose actual and symbolic labyrinths, Hamilton also unsettles viewers by literally undermining their stability. "Letting the work work on you up through your body instead of from your eyes down" is how Hamilton explained this aspect of her work a few years ago.[14] "Forcing your mind down to your legs"[15] was part of her description of an especially dramatic element of *whitecloth*, in which an eight-foot-wide circular section of the floor was made to spin in a continual clockwise motion. Viewers are invited to stand on the revolving wooden platform, though each additional body slows its rotation, ultimately to a standstill (movement resumes with the viewers' departure). At its fastest, the rotational speed is not threatening but does present, the artist admits, "a bit of a dare."[16] Hamilton has placed things underfoot before, impeding or enhancing passage with horsehair, pennies, linotype slugs, steel, and glass. Here, viewers who submit to the work's underground impulses must engage in a fairly vigorous exercise of inner balance. Mimicking (when alone) the euphoric solo spinning that, like other forms of physical transport, is associated with religious practices based in immediate personal revelation (including, in New England tradition, the early Quakers and, in turn, Shakers), viewers are also encouraged to enact, together, an image of the steadiness that comes with congregation.

In another, equally arresting act of subversion, Hamilton set a metal basin into the floor, its bottom recessed a few inches below the floorboards. As the white cloth passes in front of each of the thirteen windows, it triggers a motion detector, which in turn activates a speaker beneath the basin. This speaker generates, with a sonorous hum, a sound wave that is carried through the water in a symmetrical pattern of interlocking ripples. The most cheerfully all-American, magical-mechanical, contraption-loving element of the installation (affinities range from Rube Goldberg and Buster Keaton to contemporary artists including Charles Ray), this work is, at the same time, one of the show's most mournful. Like condensation on a cold surface, the drum of water materializes a fugitive state, capturing the white flag and with it a bit of reticent, implicit melodrama: the image is of a spinster's brief (and endlessly repeated) wave at the window, with its momentary occlusion of sunlight; from inside the house comes the deep, responding shudder, final (each time) as a stone dropped in a well. The profoundly ambivalent tact of this gesture, its voluble silence, speaks for the complex character of traditional femininity, passionate but repressed, that Hamilton identifies with The Aldrich building, but it has echoes in her own previous work as well.

We needed fire to make
the tongs and tongs to hold
us from the flame; we needed
ash to clean the cloth
and cloth to clean the ash's
stain; we needed stars
to find our way, to make
the light that blurred the stars;
we needed death to mark
an end, an end that time
in time could mend.
Born in love, the consequence –
born of love, the need.
Tell me, ravaged singer,
how the cinder bears the seed.

Susan Stewart
"Cinder" (from *The Forest*)

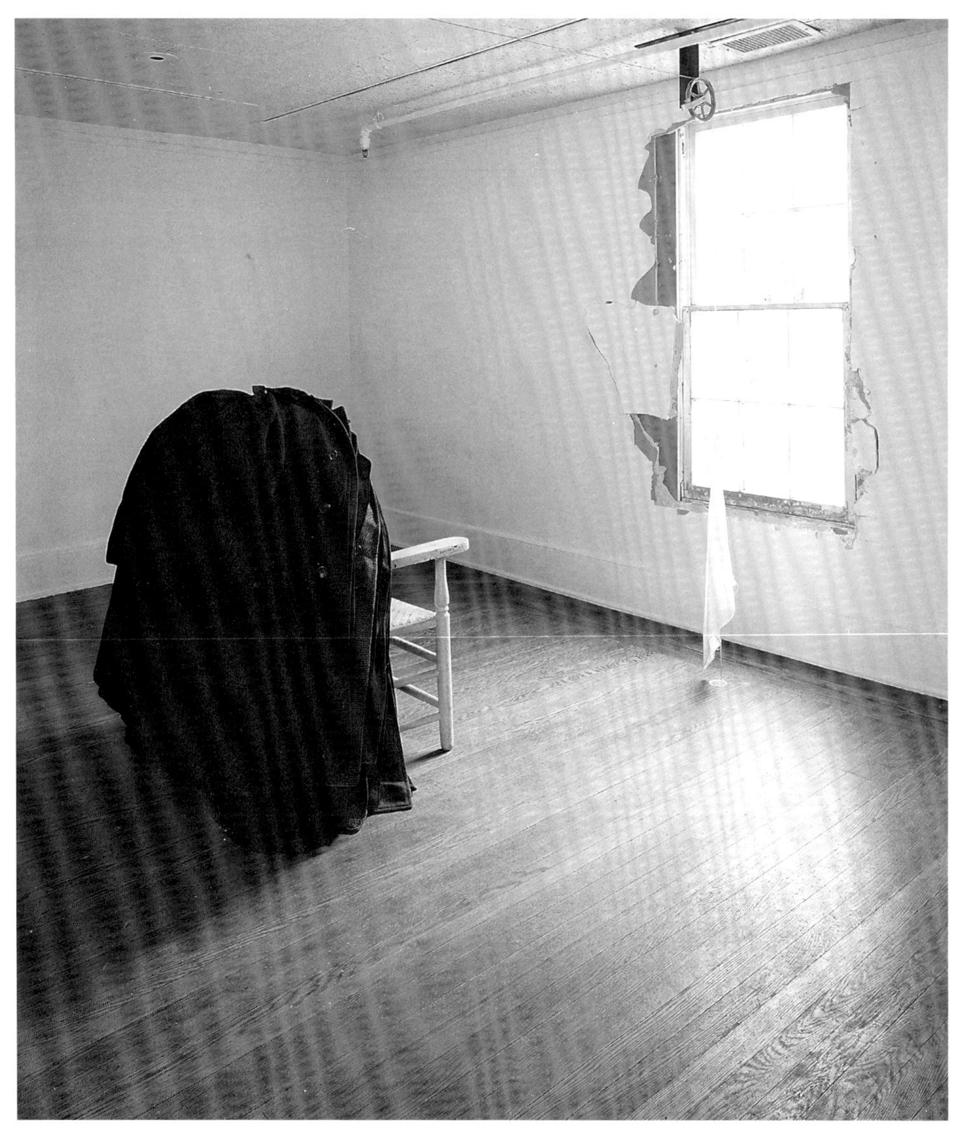

Describing an installation made more than ten years ago, in which speaking into one of 150 microphones stilled the water swirling in one of as many glasses,[17] she said, with characteristic eloquence, "I thought about how when we speak we still the internal vortex of thought."[18]

In the room directly above the water-filled drum, Hamilton created, for *whitecloth*, a new version of *welle*,[19] the "weeping wall" in which tiny beads of water emerge from nearly undetectable pores and trickle slowly down the white surface. Seemingly solid but demonstrably permeable—like cloth, and skin, and the old false walls of The Aldrich—*welle* is across the hallway from an old chair, standing empty in front of a window, and draped with layers of men's overcoats. A relic of a previous installation,[20] the chair here serves as an image of labor, figuratively anticipating *welle*'s sweat. Set into another wall is a videotape of a mysterious, sensual repetitive movement (it is a pocketful of seeping honey, manipulated by an unseen hand), extending the installation's range of involuntary, hypnotically repeated physical acts. Several other small works are (like the inscribed thimble) original to this exhibition: a big, vicious-looking clown collar, its rigid folds made of mirror-bright metal, is displayed in the same room as the revolving floor. Rhyming formally with that work, it also suggests a related experience of physical dissociation, since the wearer would be unable to see his or her body below. Upstairs is a tiny photograph, blurry and at first illegible, though it seems to show a single, staring eye. In fact, it is the artist's mouth, seen from within: placing a miniature pinhole camera inside her lips, and exposing its film by simply opening her mouth, Hamilton caught her own face reflected in a round hand-mirror—in the little photo, the reflection looks like the apparent eye's iris. Here the stilled voice (it is muted by the camera) is replaced with an image, unassuming but hungry. Describing a previous work in terms remarkably pertinent to this image, Hamilton spoke of "interiors which are also exteriors," and said that in an attempt to assimilate them, "Our eyes have become voracious like mouths."[21]

One final work, small and delicate, its position in the exhibition uncertain until the last minute, helps summarize *whitecloth's* themes. Though she originally meant it to be a single hand muff, made of stiff black organza, Hamilton decided to split this sculpture in two; as she had intended from the start, each half was lined with the form of a hand (an inner 'glove'). Even if placed side by side, the length of the muff segments would prohibit inserted hands from touching each other; as it is, the two halves are installed on separate shelves, on separate floors of the Museum. An elegant, tastefully beribboned image of frustration and isolation, of physical disjunction and, by allusion, psychological alienation, this divided sculpture also suggests—with altogether seemly, Victorian modesty—the opportunity for enhanced sensual self-awareness. Above all, it is a work of resistance to psychological resolution, one element in a composite portrait of a figure luminous and finely wrought but fragmented beyond the possibility of univocal coherence. Talking of this sculpture while it was in progress, Hamilton said, "The space between," where the fingertips in the gloves are prevented from touching each other, "is what the show is about."[22]

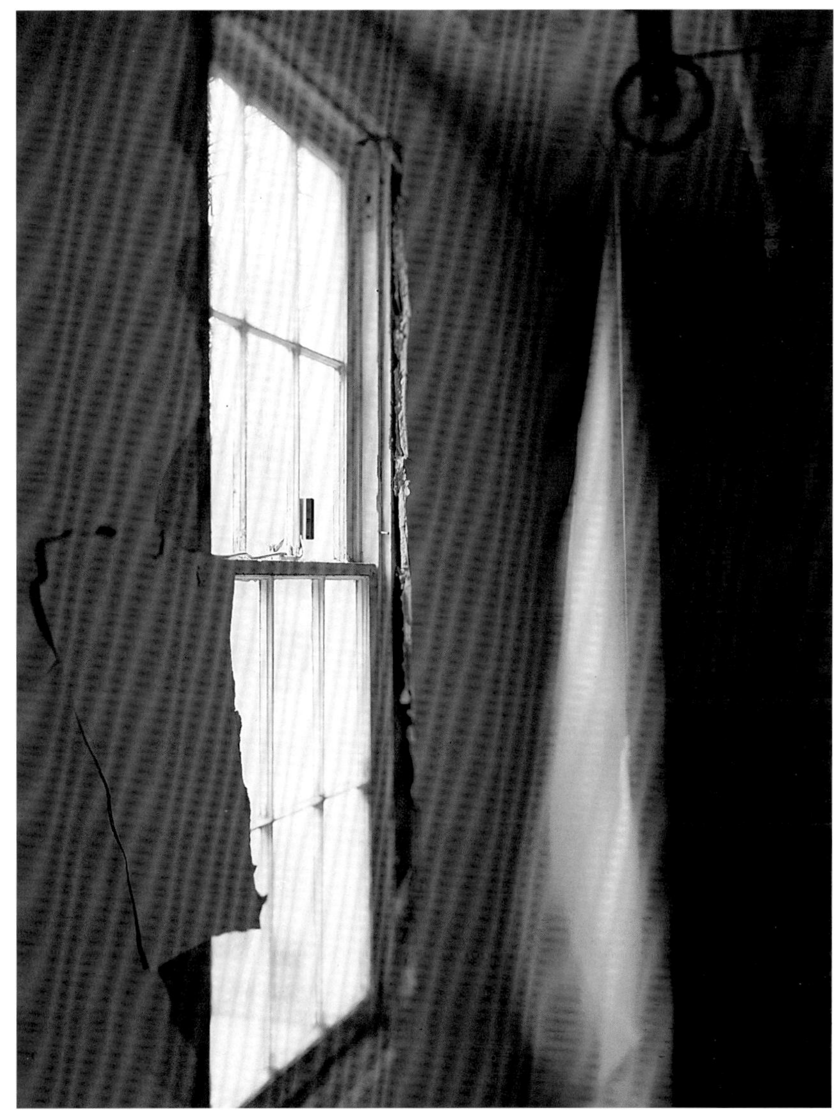

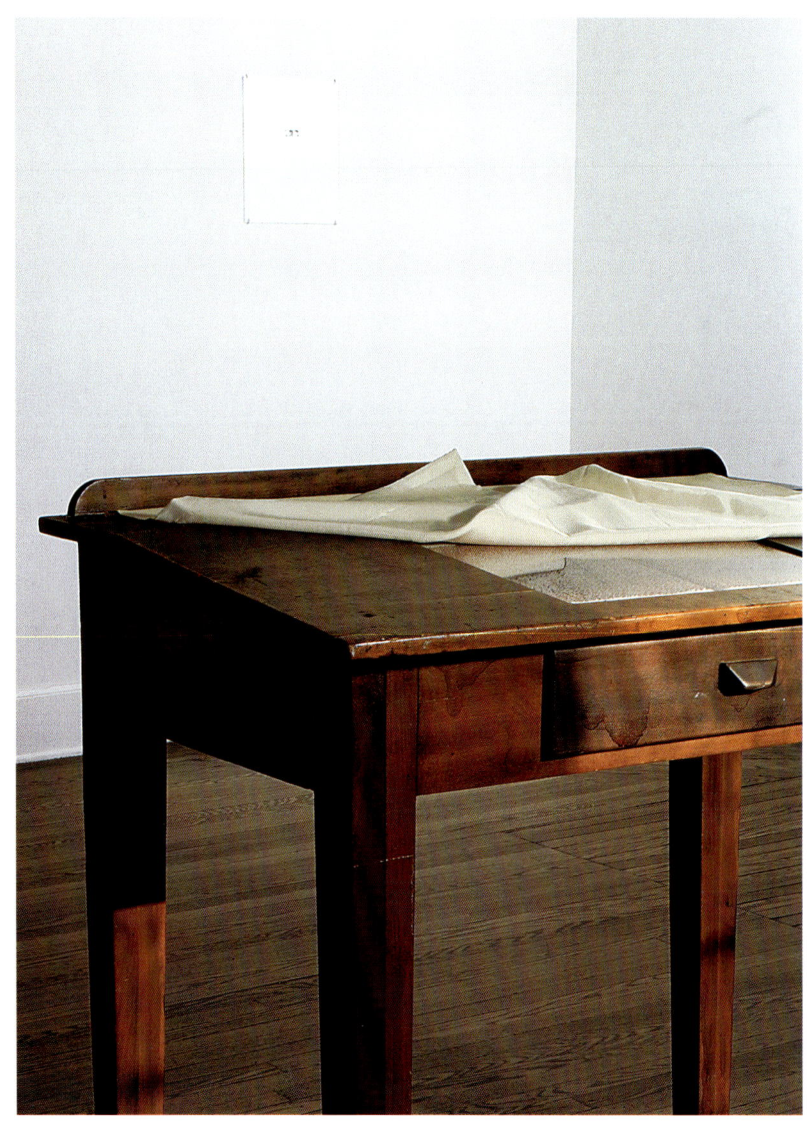

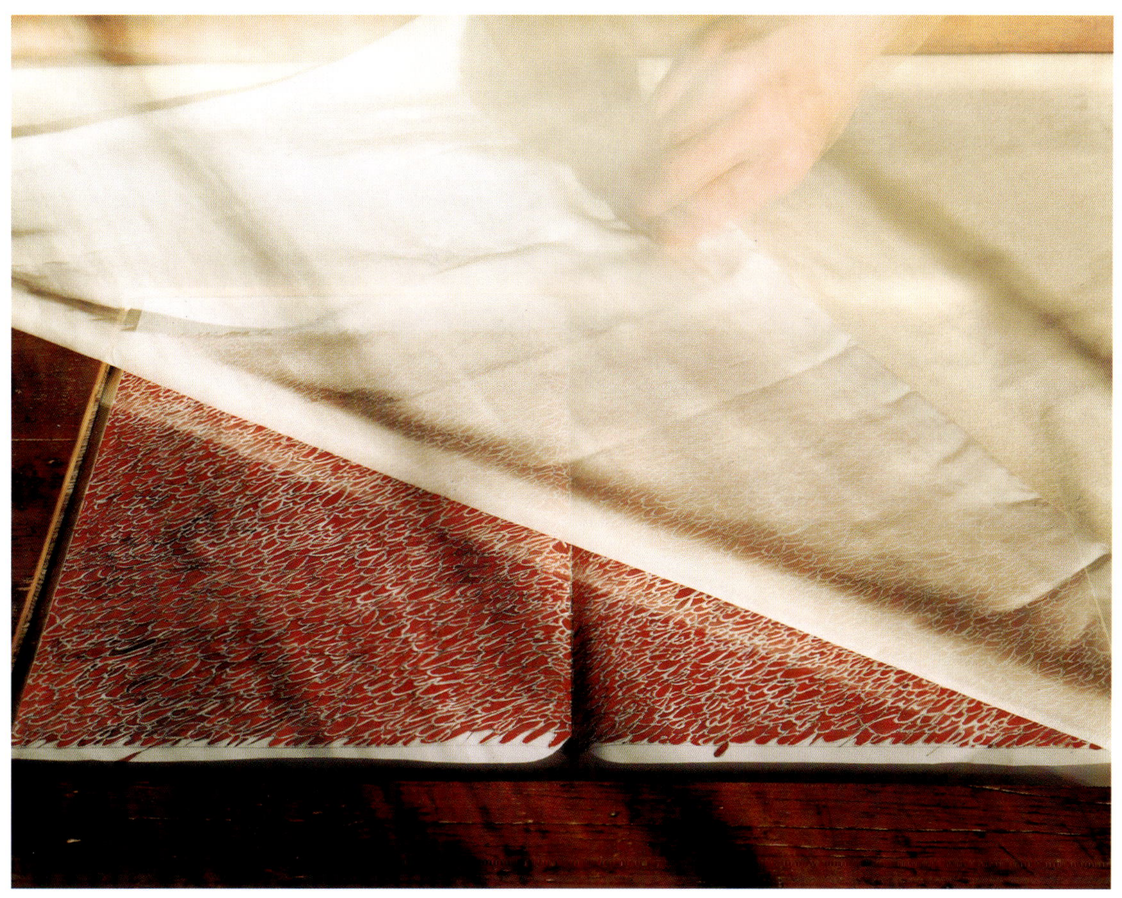

NOTES

1. Ann Hamilton, from remarks made at the reception for the opening of *whitecloth*, 24 January 1999.
2. Hamilton, quoted in Neville Wakefield, "Ann Hamilton: Between Words and Things," *Ann Hamilton: mneme*, ed. Judith Nesbitt (Liverpool: Tate Gallery, 1994), 16.
3. Leo Steinberg, "Other Criteria," in *Other Criteria: Confrontations with Twentieth Century Art* (London and Oxford: Oxford University Press, 1972), 82–91.
4. Philip Fisher, *Making and Effacing Art: Modern American Art in a Culture of Museums* (Cambridge and London: Harvard University Press, 1991), 150.
5. Hamilton did not use the addition made to the building in 1987.
6. Susan Howe, *The Birth-mark: unsettling the wilderness in American Literary History* (Hanover and London: Wesleyan University Press, 1993), 11. The more traditional historian Perry Miller wrote (in 1939), "Antinomianism was an uncontrolled piety without the indispensable ballast of reason; Puritanism looked upon itself as the synthesis of piety and reason." *The New England Mind: The 17th Century* (Boston: Beacon Press, 1964), 373.
7. Howe, *The Birth-mark*, 52.
8. Hamilton, quoted in Carey Lovelace, "Ann Hamilton," *Art News*, May 1997, 142.
9. Hamilton, in an interview with Aldrich Museum curator of education Nina Carlson, in an unpaginated exhibition brochure (Aldrich Museum, 1999).
10. Hamilton, in a discussion with the author, January 1999.
11. In Modernist art, Fisher writes, "An object is produced whose content is not an image but the instructions for setting it in historical relations," as represented by museums. *Making and Effacing Art*, 35.
12. In Hamilton's installations, *tropos* (1998), *indigo blue* (1991), and an untitled multiple (1992), respectively.
13. It was first installed as part of *reserve* (1996), at the van Abbemuseum, Eindhoven.
14. Hamilton, in an interview with Joan Simon, "The Third Lyons Biennale of Contemporary Art, Ann Hamilton: Temporal Crossroads," *Art Press* 208 (December 1995), 24.
15. Hamilton, remarks, 24 January 1999.
16. Hamilton, remarks, 24 January 1999.
17. In Hamilton's installation *the capacity of absorption* (1988), Los Angeles Museum of Contemporary Art.
18. Interview with Joan Simon, *Art Press* 208, 30.
19. Other versions of *welle* (1997), were installed at P.S. 1 in New York, Cartier Foundation in Paris, and as part of *bounden* (1997), Musée d'Art Contemporain in Lyons.
20. The chair was part of *mantle* (1998), at the Miami Art Museum; during the exhibition, a pile of "flayed" coats, their seams all cut apart, were laboriously re-stitched and placed one by one on this chair.
21. Interview with Joan Simon, *Art Press* 208, 29.
22. Hamilton, in a conversation with the author, January 1999.

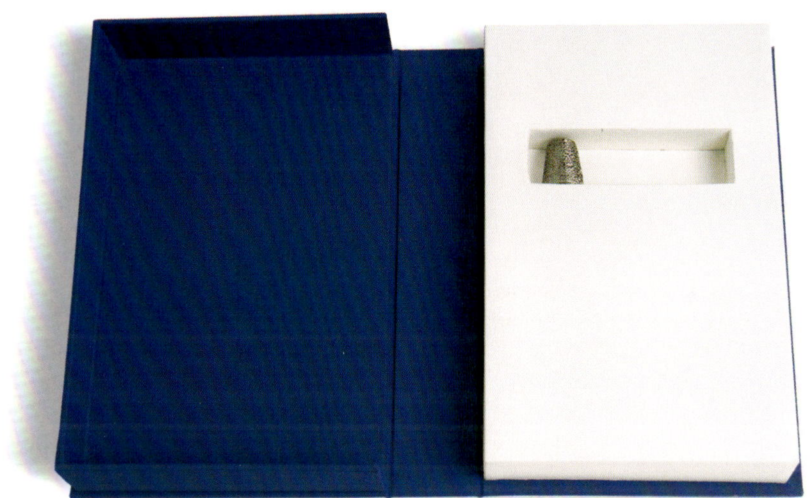

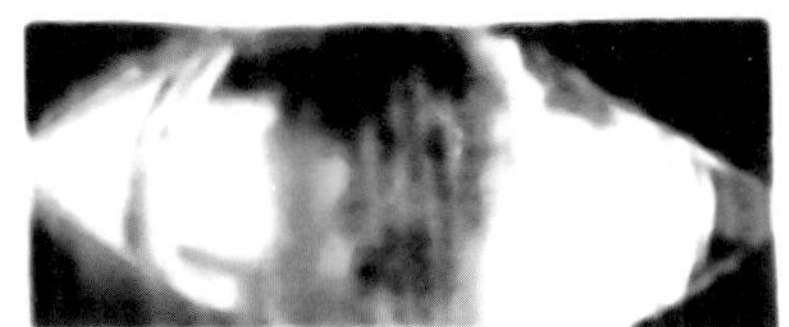

whitecloth, 1999

Mixed-media installation: electrical and mechanical components, wood, silk, glass, metal, video, water, drawing, photography and found objects

Courtesy Sean Kelly, New York

Photo credits:
Lynda Carroll: pages 10, 12, 14, 16, 18, 22, 24, 26, 28, 30, 32, 34
Liz Deschenes: pages 43, 60, 65
Hester + Hardaway: page 56 (detail)
Thibault Jeanson: Cover, frontispiece, pages 41, 52, 56 (overall view), 63
Sean Scully: page 4
Steve Willard: pages 8, 37, 40, 42, 46, 47, 48, 49, 50, 64

The Aldrich Museum of Contemporary Art

Founded 1964

CHAIRMAN'S CIRCLE

Mr. and Mrs. Larry Aldrich
Alexander Julian Foundation for Aesthetic Understanding and Appreciation
Emily and Richard Buckingham
Connecticut Commission on the Arts
Teresa and Jeffrey Furman – Fortrend International, LLC
Anna-Maria and Stephen M. Kellen
Mr. Henry Leir
Lini and Louis J. Lipton
Sherry Hope and Joel Mallin
Mr. Douglas F. Maxwell
O'Grady Family Foundation
Sheila and Charles Perrin Perrin Family Foundation
RJR Nabisco, Inc.
Martin and Toni Sosnoff Foundation
Sotheby's
Drs. Marc J. and Livia Straus
Genevieve and Richard Tucker
Judy and Peter Wasserman

BENEFACTOR

Walter H. Annenberg, Harriett Ames Charitable Trust
Dede and James Bartlett
étant dónnes, The French American Endowment for Contemporary Art
Carol and Arthur Goldberg
Sunny and Brad Goldberg
Sandy and Leonard Gubar
Shelby White and Leon Levy
Mr. Perry J. Lewis and Basha Szymanska
Ms. Vera List
Pepsi-Cola Co.
Mr. and Mrs. F. F. Randolph, Jr.
The Reader's Digest Art Collection
Mr. and Mrs. Warren Rubin – Workbench, Inc. of Greenwich, Westport, Scarsdale & Danbury
Dr. and Mrs. Harvey Sadow

PATRON

Ann and Steven Ames
Caroline and Richard Anderson
Atalanta/Sosnoff Capital Corp.
Frank E. Baxter
Boehringer Ingelheim Corp.
Marianne Boesky Fine Art
Alice Saligman and Klaus Brinkman
Dr. Brian Clark – Schlumberger-Doll Research
Mr. Stephen B. Brown
David R. Collens – Storm King Art Center
Patton R. Corrigan – The Stamford Capital Group, Inc.
Jeanne and Richard Fisher
Joyce Lowinson Kootz and Helmut N. Friedlaender
Mindy and Laurence Friedman
Pamela and Robert Goergen – The Ropart Group
Marianne Goodman Gallery
The Gordon F Linke and Jocelyn B Linke Foundation
Mr. and Mrs. Gregory Holt, – Daybrook Resources, Corp.
Housatonic Valley Travel Commission
Jill and Ken Iscol

Katonah Art Museum
Mary and Robert Kidder
Sandy and Harlan P. Kleiman
Carolyn Labutka –
AON Foundation
Jo Carole and Ronald S. Lauder
Mr. Peter Malkin
Marlborough Gallery
Carol and Raymond Merritt
Robert Miller Gallery
Deanne and Richard Mincer
Mr. and Mrs. Jerry Minsky
Mr. and Mrs. Lester Morse, Jr. –
Morse Family Foundation
Nash Family Foundation, Inc.
Ann and Martin Rabinowitz
Ridgefield Bank
The Richard and Hinda
Rosenthal Foundation
Saks Fifth Avenue
Samuel Zell Foundation
Hannelore and R. B. Schulhof
Agnes Gund and Daniel Shapiro
Renate and Sidney Shapiro
Dr. and Mrs. Robert Soley
Mr. Arthur Stern III
Mr. and Mrs. Anthony Ullmann
Jean and David Wallace
Mr. Leonard Wien
Mr. and Mrs. Mark Wheless

DIRECTOR'S CIRCLE

Mr. and Mrs. Ralph Ablon
Mr. and Mrs. Stefan Abrams
Jill Weinberg Adams and
Thomas Adams –
Lennon, Weinberg, Inc.
Glenn Bailey
Madeleine and Jay Bennett
Bonakdar Jancou Gallery
Mr. Henry Buhl, III
Chancellor Park at Laurelwood
Eileen and Michael Cohen
Paula Cooper Gallery
Zoe and Joel Dictrow
Phyllis and Donald Duberstein
Mr. Martin Edelston –
Boardroom, Inc.
Jody and Stuart Eichner
Andre Emmerich Gallery
Gail and Al Engelberg
Ursula and Peter Evans
Nancy and A. Robert Faesy
Ronald Feldman Gallery
Joni Weyl and Sidney Felsen –
Gemini G.E.L.
Cheryl and Robert Fishko –
Forum Gallery
Mr. and Mrs. Joel Freedman
Eve and Theodore Friedman
Galerie LeLong
Barbara Gladstone Gallery
Robert Gober
Mr. and Mrs. Stuart Green
Ursula Von Rydinsvard and
Paul Greengard
Mr. Leo Guthman
Mr. Andrew Hall
Barbara and Rod R. Hamachek
Barbara Handman,
People for the American Way
Mr. Peter Hoffman –
Duracell International Inc.
Mr. Rolf Heitmeyer
Mr. and Mrs. Paul L. Herring
Mr. and Mrs. Harry Huberth
Ms. Nash Hyon
Mr. Robert Kidder
Hedy and Kent Klineman
Werner Kramarsky
Luhring Augustine Gallery
Susan and David Marco
Bill Maynes Gallery
Marlborough Gallery
Robert Miller Gallery
Mr. Roger Mudre –
The Ridgefield Guild of Artists
New York Community Trust
Mr. and Mrs. Walter Northup
PaceWildenstein
People's Bank
Ellen and Robert Perless
Yvonne and Leslie Pollack
Marianne and Ed Pollak
Nancy and Joel Portney
Andrea and Andrew Potash
Mr. and Mrs. Alan Safir
St. Onge, Steward, Johnston & Reens
Mr. Stanley B. Scheinman
Stephen Haller Gallery, Inc.
Barbara Schwartz
Stephanie and Abram Shnay
Sheila and Ramsey Siegel
Sue and Marco Stoffel
Mr. Laurie Tisch Sussman
Mark Theran

MUSEUM STAFF

Jonathan Bodge
Preparator

Nancy Bradbury
Office Assistant

Nina Carlson
Curator of Education

Lynda James Carroll
Associate Curator of Education

Rafe Churchill
Associate Curator of Education

Suzanne Enser-Ryan
Music Coordinator

Paul Harrick
Facilities Manager

Heide Hendricks
Director of Public Affairs

Jessica Hough
Assistant Curator

Richard Klein
Assistant Director

Jennifer Millett-Barrett
Membership Coordinator

Anne Murphy
Event and Gallery Manager

Wendy Northup Moran
Volunteer Coordinator

Harry Philbrick
Director

Robin G. Phillips
Accounting

Barbara Toplin
Volunteer Museum Store Manager

Kay Usher
Museum Secretary

Aran Winterbottom
Public Relations Assistant

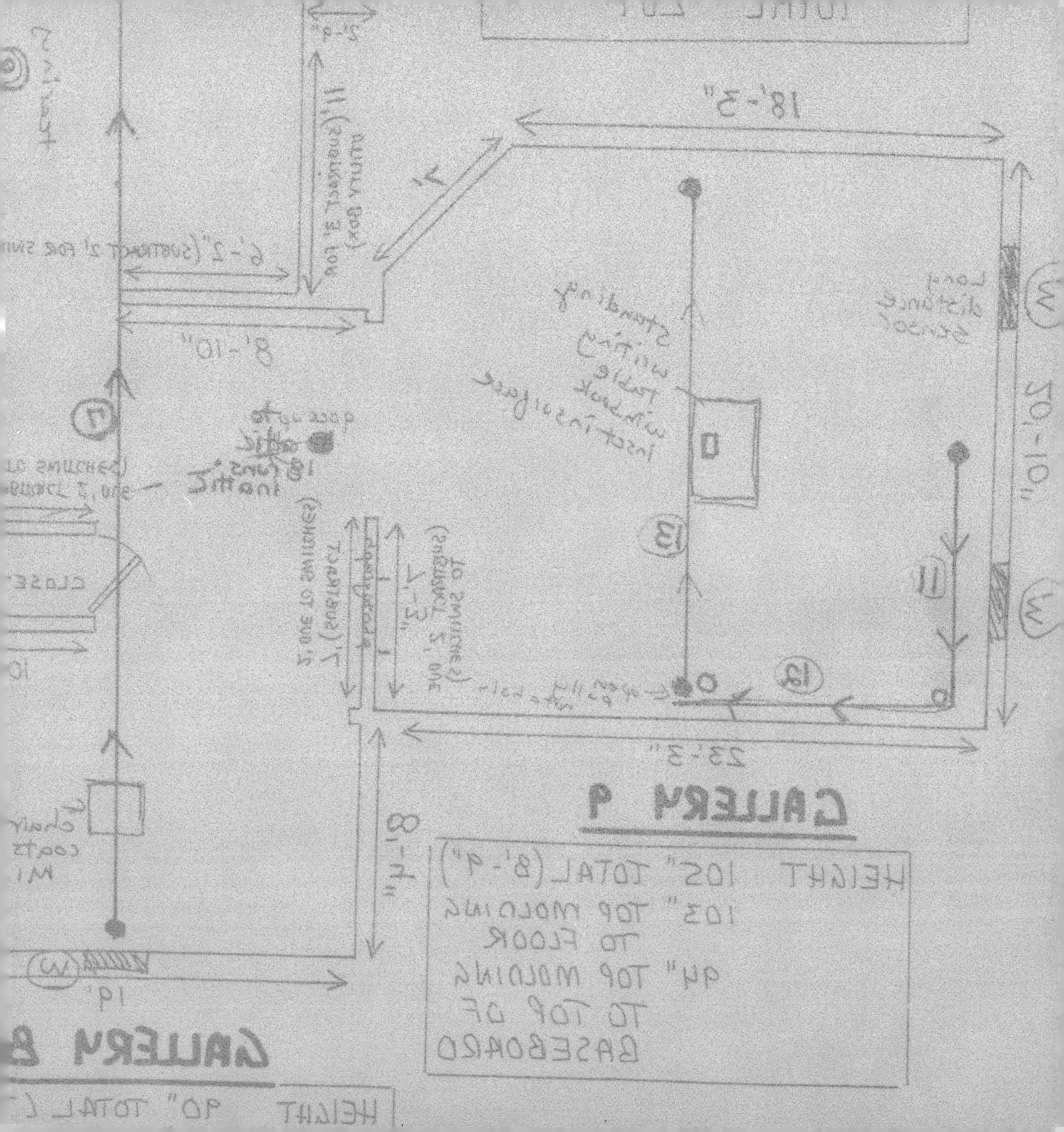

18'-3"
7'
8'-10"
6'-2" (SUBTRACT 2' FOR
standing writing table w/ insect in surface
long distance sensor
20'-10"
23'-3"
8'-4"
GALLERY 9
HEIGHT 105" TOTAL (8'-9")
103" TOP MOLDING TO FLOOR
94" TOP MOLDING TO TOP OF BASEBOARD
14'
GALLERY 8
HEIGHT 90" TOTAL (
CLOSET

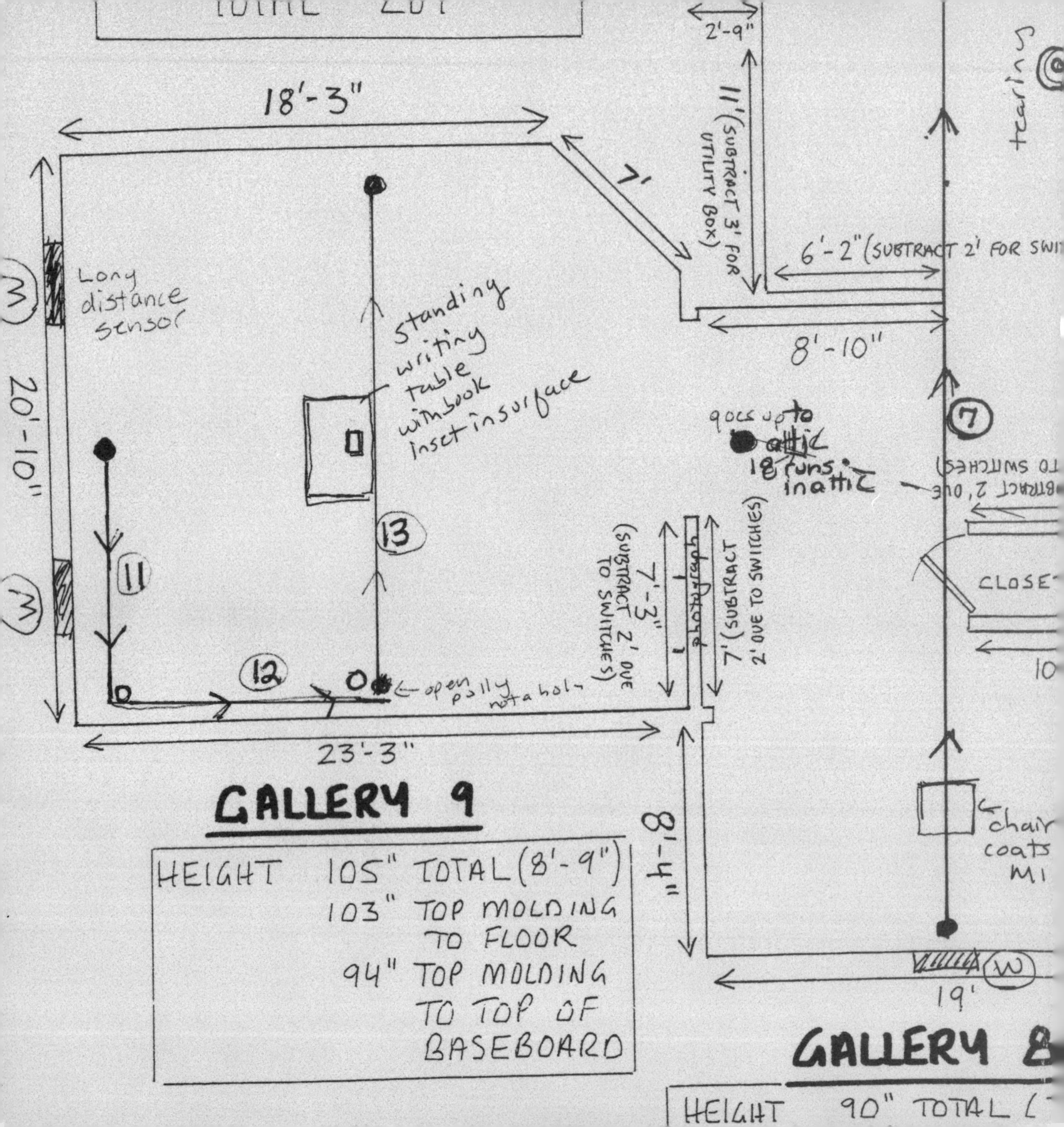

18'-3"
7'
2'-9"
11' (SUBTRACT 3' FOR UTILITY BOX)
6'-2" (SUBTRACT 2' FOR SWI
8'-10"
Long distance sensor
20'-10"
standing writing table with book inset in surface
goes up to attic
18 runs in attic
TO SWITCHES
SUBTRACT 2' DUE
7
13
11
12
open pully not a hole
7'-3" (SUBTRACT 2' DUE TO SWITCHES)
7' (SUBTRACT 2' DUE TO SWITCHES)
CLOSE
10
23'-3"
GALLERY 9
HEIGHT 105" TOTAL (8'-9")
103" TOP MOLDING TO FLOOR
94" TOP MOLDING TO TOP OF BASEBOARD
8'-4"
chair coats
19'
GALLERY 8
HEIGHT 90" TOTAL